The South Downs

A DOG WALKER'S GUIDE

Tracey Gower

COUNTRYSIDE BOOKS
NEWBURY BERKSHIRE

COUNTRYSIDE BOOKS
3 Catherine Road
Newbury, Berkshire

To view our complete range of books,
please visit us at
www.countrysidebooks.co.uk

ISBN 978 1 84674 368 9

The cover picture shows a dog walker enjoying the South Downs
at Devil's Dyke by Simon Dack News/Alamy

Designed and Typeset by KT Designs, St Helens
Produced through The Letterworks Ltd., Reading
Printed by The Holywell Press, Oxford

Contents

Walk

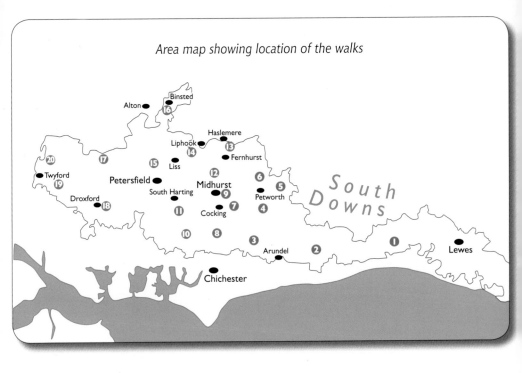

Area map showing location of the walks

PUBLISHER'S NOTE

We hope that you obtain considerable enjoyment from this book; great care has been taken in its preparation. Although at the time of publication all routes followed public rights of way or permitted paths, diversion orders can be made and permissions withdrawn. We cannot, of course, be held responsible for such diversion orders and any inaccuracies in the text which result from these or any other changes to the routes, or any damage which might result from walkers trespassing on private property. We are anxious, though, that all details relating to the walks are kept up to date, and would therefore welcome information from readers which would be relevant to future editions.

The simple sketch maps that accompany the walks in this book are based on notes made by the author whilst checking out the routes on the ground. They are designed to show you how to reach the start and to point out the main features of the overall circuit, and they contain a progression of numbers that relate to the paragraphs of the text.

However, for the benefit of a proper map, we do recommend that you purchase the relevant Ordnance Survey sheet covering your walk. The Ordnance Survey maps are widely available, especially through booksellers and local newsagents.

INTRODUCTION

From rolling hills to bustling market towns, the South Downs National Park's landscape covers 1,600 square kilometres of breathtaking views and hidden gems.

When I was asked to compile a book of dog-friendly walks within the South Downs National Park, I had no idea that in doing so I would learn so much about the beautiful area I am lucky enough to live in. Having walked and ridden here decades before it became a National Park in 2011, I now realise that I had hardly scratched the surface of what this area has to offer for days out with our dogs.

The area is vast, and with so many dog-friendly places to choose, keeping it down to just 20 walks was so difficult that this book covers routes in just the western and central part of the park. I have tried to show with the selection of walks how this side of the park is so much more than the South Downs. As well as the beautiful chalk grassland and forestry of the Downs, the walks cover open farmland, wooded hangers, and important heathland, most of which is part of a conservation project called Heathlands Reunited, led by the South Downs National Park Authority (www.southdowns.gov.uk). The routes often follow, in part, the courses of long-distance national paths.

I hope you will agree that all of the routes I have chosen for the book are pleasant walks in any season. Many of the walks cross open-access land. Why not use the route to get your bearings, and then, if you are still in the area, return to explore more?

Tracey Gower

Acknowledgements

I would like to thank all my clients at k9-antics who, while cheerfully helping me check the 'dog friendliness' (or not, in some cases) of walking routes, gave me an insight into other people's views of what makes a good dog walk. My own dogs all loved being 'testers'. Boris, in particular, being young, large and goofy, was chief stile and refreshment tester.

ADVICE FOR DOG WALKERS

It is good practice to follow the Countryside Code when walking anywhere in the countryside. There are five sections of the Code dedicated to helping members of the public respect, protect and enjoy the countryside.

- Be safe, plan ahead and follow the footpath signs.
- Leave gates and property as you find them.
- Protect plants and animals and take your litter home.
- Keep dogs under close control, especially near farm animals and during nesting season.
- Consider other people.

The South Downs National Park Authority welcomes responsible dog owners and has their own educational campaign called 'Take the Lead'. For further information, visit www.southdowns.gov.uk/enjoy/take-the-lead.

When walking your dog in the South Downs:

- Keep dogs on a lead near livestock. If a farm animal chases you and your dog, it is safer to let your dog off the lead – don't risk getting hurt by trying to protect it. Remember, your dog can run faster than you!
- Bag and bin your dog's poo – any public bin will do. Everyone knows how unpleasant dog mess is, and it can cause infections, so always clean up after your dog and get rid of the mess responsibly. Also make sure your dog is wormed regularly to protect it, other animals and people.
- Protect ground-nesting birds. Stick to the paths, especially between 1st March and 15th September, and make sure your dog doesn't wander where it might disturb birds that nest on the ground and other wildlife – eggs and young will soon die without protection from their parents.
- Do not enter military training areas when the red flags are flying.

Adders

Many of the walks are across heathland, which is home to adders. The adder is a timid and non-aggressive snake, and will only bite when provoked. They hibernate over the winter, emerging in early spring as the ambient temperature increases. They are all recognizable by their dorsal zigzag pattern, with a V or X shape on the head. Most adder bites occur between April and July.

What should you do if your dog is bitten?

Most importantly, **do not panic**: your dog is highly likely to make a full recovery if treated promptly and correctly.

- If your dog is bitten, minimise their movement and seek veterinary attention without delay.

- The most common signs are significant swelling local to the bite, with systemic signs of depression and lethargy.

- 96–97% make a full recovery, usually within five days.

Poisoning

Many garden and agricultural chemicals can be attractive to dogs, but they can be fatal, so never let your dog out of sight or let it eat what it finds when out for a walk. If you think your dog has ingested something poisonous, phone the vet immediately, and keep any labels, containers or samples with you to help the vet decide the best treatment. Do not make your dog sick without first consulting the vet.

Heat stroke

Heat stroke occurs when dogs are exercised in hot weather, or left in cars on even moderately warm days. They will pant excessively and may vomit, collapse, and have fits or difficulty breathing. If heat stroke occurs:

- Keep the dog calm. Move it into the shade, a cool building or room, or near a fan or breeze.

- Cool your dog with water, paying particular attention to the head.

- Let your dog drink small amounts of cool water frequently. Call a vet.

As a dog trainer and behaviourist, I also believe it is good practice to call your dog close or pop the lead on when you see horses, cyclists, young children or other dogs on leads. This will help to keep everyone safe. It can be really useful to take the time to teach your dog how to negotiate stiles and narrow bridges before they meet one in a strange place. Most of the walks in the book give the dogs plenty of opportunity to run free, but this is dependent on having a good recall.

Well, that's the serious bit out of the way. Now enjoy a guided doggie roam around some of the best places in England for walking your dog.

Devil's Dyke
4 miles (6.4 km)

Devil's Dyke.

The **Devil's Dyke is a V-shaped valley** and the largest chalkland 'dry' combe in Britain. An Area of Outstanding Natural Beauty, it is home to many interesting plants and butterflies. In 1892, the area was turned into a Victorian version of what we would call a theme park, complete with fairground rides, and 1894 saw the opening of Britain's first aerial cableway – now long gone, but the remains of the concrete bases can still be seen. You won't see any fairground rides these days, either, but if you are walking at the weekend, you may get to watch the hang-gliders riding the wind.

The route follows a bridleway to the Iron Age hillfort where the funfair used to be, but the main attractions will undoubtedly be the amazing panoramic views across the valley.

The South Downs – A Dog Walker's Guide

How to get there & where to park

From the junction of the A23 and the A27 north of Brighton, follow the A27 west, and take the Hove exit, which is after about a mile. Here, head north on Devil's Dyke Road, signposted to Devil's Dyke. Follow the road as it bears left after about ½ mile, ignoring the road to the right. Keep to the road as it passes the Dyke Golf Club, take a sharp right bend, and you will arrive at the National Trust car park on the left after approximately ½ mile. **Sat nav** BN1 8YJ.

OS map

Explorer OL11 Brighton & Hove (GR TQ 269111).

Nearest refreshments

The Devil's Dyke pub is only a very short detour from the route. It is dog-friendly but can get busy. BN1 8YJ ☎ 01273 857256 www.vintageinn.co.uk. The grass bank on the other side of the car park fence is a lovely place for a picnic if you want to take one with you.

Dog factors

Terrain: Mainly grassland or woodland tracks. A couple of long uphill and downhill sections which get fairly steep.
Road walking: None.
Livestock: Horses on the bridleways.
Stiles: None.
Nearest vet: Ark Veterinary Group, 44 Keymer Road, Hassocks, West Sussex, BN6 8AR ☎ 01273 844399.

The Walk

1 From the car park, go through the gate in the right-hand corner, then turn left to follow the car park fence line, carrying straight on to the **South Downs Way** (SDW). Follow the SDW along a mainly level treeline track until you get to the head of the valley that is the **Devil's Dyke**.

2 Here, you will leave the SDW and drop down into the valley before heading straight up the other side to a gate. Go through the gate, and climb a little further to take the second track to the right; start walking around the hillfort. Along this path, you get a good view into the valley until the path swings uphill to the left. Keep to the path that runs around the top edge of the

hill, passing a stile on your right, before the path swings to the left towards another **National Trust car park** and the **Devil's Dyke pub**.

The views from the hilltop are outstanding so be careful not to miss the kissing gate on your right, opposite the car park.

❸ Go through the gate, and pick up a very narrow path that bears right to gradually take you down the side of the steep escarpment.

With the steep drop from the left side of the narrow path, you will need to be careful of your footing, particularly if you have to pass anyone coming up.

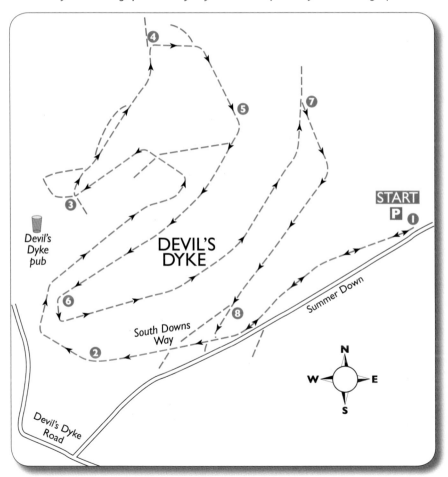

The South Downs – A Dog Walker's Guide

As the path reaches the woodland, the descent gets steeper and goes down 63 steps to a gate.

4 Bearing right through the gate, follow the permissive path through the woods to a bridleway. Turn right onto the bridleway and follow it uphill. The path will get steeper as you climb up through the woods to another gate.

5 Go through the gate to reach open grassland again. Ignore the footpaths and stay with the bridleway as it continues uphill, then curves right, before reaching a gate back onto the hillfort. Through the gate, you will find yourself on a path just below the one you walked on your outward trip around the fort, with the **Devil's Dyke** below you to your left.

6 At the end of the path, turn left to go back through the gate into the **Dyke**. This time, instead of crossing the head of the valley, drop down and turn left to walk along the floor of the valley.

7 Towards the end of the valley, the path curves left; at the apex of the turn, you turn sharply right to pick up the bridleway that runs up the other side of the valley. As you near the top, keep left where the bridleway divides.

8 At the top of the hill, the bridleway joins the **SDW**. Turn left to retrace your steps back to the car park.

Angmering Park Estate to Patching Hill
5 miles (8 km)

Springtime on the Angmering estate.

The **Angmering Park Estate is a private** agricultural and sporting estate which extends to around 6,750 acres, with a stud farm at its centre. This quiet route takes in the wide drives, the many forest tracks and bridleways, and the mature woodland of the estate. Visit in the spring if you want to see the carpet of bluebells that covers much of the woodland floor. You will also get a chance to admire the panoramic view from the grassland at the top of Patching Hill. Dogs with good recall can be off lead for nearly all of the walk.

How to get there & where to park

The Dover Lane car park can only be reached from the eastbound lane of the A27. After the road becomes dual carriageway at Crossbush, take the second turn on the left; this is just after a lay-by and signed Dover Lane. Drive ½ mile to the car park. **Sat nav** BN18 9PX.

OS map

Explorer OL10 Arundel & Pulborough (GR TQ 061065).

Nearest refreshments

The Worlds End pub on Arundel Road in Patching is a lovely, dog-friendly pub serving good food. BN13 3UQ ☎ 01903 871346. www.worldsendpatching.co.uk.

Dog factors

Terrain: Mainly easy walking, with a few gentle inclines. The bridleways can be muddy after very wet spells.

Road walking: No roads as such, but some tarmac drives where you may encounter vehicles. Angmering Park is a working country estate, so the odd vehicle is also possible on some of the forest tracks and bridleways.

Livestock: Horses and riders on the bridleways and park drives. The horses are likely to be young racehorses and may be scared by loose dogs. Cattle graze on Patching Hill.

Stiles: None.

Nearest vet: Fitzalan House Veterinary Group, 2 Church Hill, Angmering. BN16 4EG ☎ 01903 770437 (out of hours ☎ 01903 713806).

The Walk

As you drive into the car park, look for the large footpath notice to the far left of the entrance. When you have parked up, this notice is the walk's starting point.

1 At the footpath notice, turn left out of the corner of the car park to a signpost. Take the bridleway opposite, which soon bears left between fields. At the next junction, turn right, passing houses and grass paddocks. Stay with this bridleway as it merges onto an estate drive, keeping fairly straight ahead and ignoring the footpaths that join the bridleway. The drive goes gently uphill and bears right to a junction with a tarmac drive near the brow of the hill.

② Turn right. You are now on the **Monarch's Way**. The tarmac drive ends at some estate buildings. The route, following the **Monarch's Way**, continues past the buildings and keeps straight ahead onto a wide forest track. Stay on the **Monarch's Way**, which follows a fairly level, hard forest track.

③ When you reach a signpost on your right, you need to be careful that you keep following the **Monarch's Way**. The route bears left and slightly uphill for a short distance – the forest track you have been following is still fairly level. Follow the bridleway as it gently curves through the woods along the top of the **Michelgrove Park Hanger**.

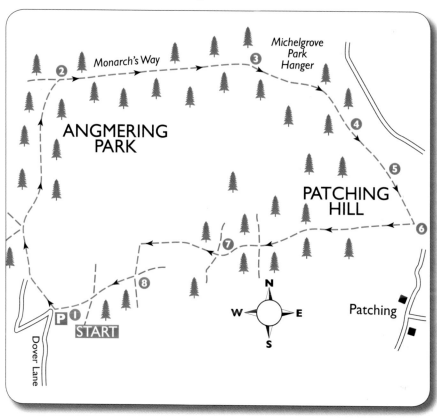

4 At the next crossroads, the Monarch's Way turns left downhill, away from our route. Stay straight ahead on the bridleway to continue along the top of the hanger to a gate exiting the **Angmering Estate**.

5 Go through the gate to reach an enclosure on the top of **Patching Hill**.

The route here can be pretty rucked up underfoot from the grazing cattle, but the panoramic views are worth it.

Walk through the enclosure to reach a gate out of the fenced area on your right.

6 Once you are through the gate, turn right along the edge of a field on a bridleway. To your left, you will have a good view of **Patching** village and beyond. The bridleway will take you into the woods, where you bear slightly right to stay on the path. As you re-enter the **Angmering Estate**, keep to the fairly straight course of this bridleway, ignoring all crossing tracks until you get to a crossroads with a hard track and a field in front of you.

7 At this junction, leave the bridleway by crossing the hard track into the field opposite. The footpath follows the edge of the wood along the headland of the field. Your view has now changed from mature woodland to open farmland, with the Downs in front of you. Just before the hedge line that separates two large fields, turn left to follow the hedge line across the field back into woodland.

8 As the footpath leaves the field, turn right to follow a bridleway once again. When the bridleway reaches a junction of tarmac estate roads, bear slightly left to continue on the road almost opposite, which will take you back to the car park.

Eartham Wood to Slindon

2¾ or 5 miles (4.4 or 8 km)

The view from Nore Hill Folly.

This enchanting walk is a favourite of mine at any time of the year, and worth revisiting as the forest colours change with the seasons. The bluebells in the spring are particularly spectacular. Eartham Wood is managed by the Forestry Commission, but the whole walk is within the National Trust-owned Slindon Estate.

The route starts in a well-managed, mature woodland with wide paths and trees that have room to grow, giving a sheltered walk with plenty of natural light. The full route is two loops connected by a short path that is walked both ways. The shorter route follows one loop and is entirely within the woodland.

The South Downs – A Dog Walker's Guide

The full route leaves the wood on the edge of the South Downs grassland at Nore Hill Folly. Built in 1814 for the Countess of Newburgh's picnic parties, the views from here do make it a lovely place to eat outdoors. The dogs can run free for all of the short route; for the longer one, they may need to be kept close around the sheep fields near the Folly.

How to get there & where to park

Turn off the A285 towards Eartham. The Eartham Woods Forestry Commission car park is on the left just before a bend in the road. **Sat nav** PO18 0LU.

OS map

Explorer OL10 Arundel & Pulborough (GR SU 938106).

Nearest refreshments

The George at Eartham is well worth a visit. Dogs are welcome inside and out, and the food is highly rated. PO18 0LT ☎ 01243 814340. www.thegeorgeeartham.com.

Dog factors

Terrain: Mainly semi-hard forest tracks with a few long inclines.
Road walking: None, but you may encounter farm or forestry vehicles.
Livestock: None other than horses and riders on the shorter route. The longer route goes past well-fenced sheep fields.
Stiles: None.
Nearest vet: Mark Elliott and Associates, Madam Green Business Centre, High Street, Oving, West Sussex, PO20 2DD ☎ 01243 779111.

The Walk

1 Start the walk at the back of the car park, directly opposite the metal barrier you drove under to get in. Pass the cut-off posts, and ignore the path to your right, instead taking the one through the avenue of trees ahead of you. Follow this path to the fence line around **Jackdine Farm**. Turn right to follow the fence line to a junction of 5 paths.

2 At the junction, turn left with the fence line, and follow the path a little way to the next path on your right. Take this right turn, and follow the straight

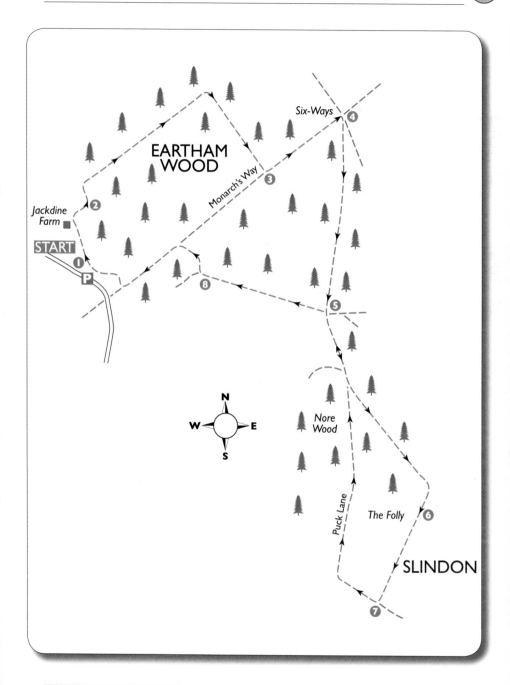

The South Downs – A Dog Walker's Guide

route until you cross over a hard track. Keep straight ahead where the soft track meets another hard track. When your way is again crossed by a hard track, turn right down the hill to a crossroads.

③ At the crossroads, join the **Monarch's Way** on **Stane Street**. Turn left, and stay on this path until you reach the junction of paths that is known as **'Six-Ways'**.

The Monarch's Way is a 615-mile long-distance path which marks the approximate route taken in 1651 by King Charles II. Defeated in the Battle of Worcester, he escaped to Brighton from Worcester via Bristol and Yeovil. The 'Six-Ways' junction gets its name from the 'Shipphams Poste', a signpost showing six destinations (where eight paths now meet). The post was donated to the National Trust by a local family of the same name.

Nore Hill Folly.

4 At the **'Six-Ways'** post, take the first right towards **Slindon**. The path you want has a green sign saying, **'NO HORSES'**. Stay on this path until you reach a junction with a bridleway just past a green metal post.

At this junction, the shorter route turns right and picks up the directions again at Point 8.

5 Crossing the bridleway, continue on the footpath uphill to another signpost next to a wooden barrier. Turn left past the wooden barrier, and start to drop downhill out of the woodland. This path ends on a track running alongside a fenced sheep field.

This is a good time to give your dog a rest from all the woodland free running and keep them close.

Turn right on the hard track. You will see grass fields to your left and open views in front of you as you drop downhill towards the Folly.

6 *It's worth taking a break at the Folly to enjoy the view, or have a picnic. On a clear day you may see the Halnaker Windmill, Portsmouth's Spinnaker Tower, Chichester Cathedral and even a glimpse of the sea at Bognor.*

Leaving the **Folly**, follow the footpath signs down to a T-junction with a hard track; this is the bridleway known as **Puck Lane**.

7 Turn right to follow the bridleway past a barn, then round a bend. Ignore the footpath that joins to the left, and stay on the bridleway as it runs uphill into **Nore Wood**.

This is a great place to see bluebells in the spring.

Near the brow of the hill, pass the wooden barrier again, and retrace your steps back to the junction at Point 5. This time, turn left to follow the bridleway along the edge of the woods.

8 When you reach a large wooden post, the path bears left, but you will leave the bridleway and turn right. This track soon curves left, taking you back to **Stane Street** and the **Monarch's Way**. Turn left, and follow the wide track to a T-junction. Turn right, away from the metal barrier, up a wide forest track, and after a few metres, you will arrive at a smaller track on your left. This will take you back to the car park.

Burton Mill Pond to Shopham Bridge
3¼ miles (5.2 km)

Burton Mill Pond.

Burton Mill Pond is a 16th-century 'hammer pond', created to provide a force of water for the watermill to drive the hammer needed in the production of iron, an important industry in the area at the time. Over the centuries, as the needs of the Burton Park Estate changed, the mill went through many conversions. Its uses included driving a turbine to provide power to the house and the more familiar use for a mill, grinding corn.

The mill building is now privately owned, but it has a few open days a year. Burton Mill Pond, along with the adjoining Chingford Pond and the heath and marshland around them, are now a Site of Special Scientific Interest managed by the Sussex Wildlife Trust. The route is mainly through the nature reserve, coming back across farmland alongside the River Rother.

Dog factors

Terrain: Mainly good, fairly flat going. Wet in places at some times of the year.

Road walking: Two short sections on quiet country lanes, and a little way along a private drive.

Livestock: The route crosses a couple of fields that may contain cows.

Stiles: Four, all easily negotiated by a large dog (Great Dane cross).

Nearest vet: Newbridge Veterinary Surgery, Wharf Farm, Wisborough Green, RH14 0JG (on the A272) ☎ 01403 784777.

How to get there & where to park
Turn off the A285 at Heath End, signposted for Burton Mill Pond. There is a small car park on the right at Burton and Chingford Ponds Nature Reserve. **Sat nav** GU28 0JR.

OS map
Explorer OL10 Arundel & Pulborough (GR SU 978180).

Nearest refreshments
The Cricketers at Duncton is a family-run, dog-friendly pub and a firm favourite of mine. GU28 0LB ☎ 01798 342473 www.thecricketersduncton.co.uk.

The Walk

❶ From the car park, walk back to the road, taking a moment to enjoy the view of **Burton Mill Pond** in front of you. Turn right after a few metres to cross the road, and turn left down the marked footpath. Very soon, you will pass through a gate into the nature reserve.

2 Go through a gate, and turn left to follow the **Serpent Trail** down a private drive. Keep fairly straight ahead past the few dwellings, and follow the drive until it turns left around the end of a large green. Continue on the **Serpent Trail** as it continues straight onto a hard track, passing through another gate. This track takes you over the spillway where **Chingford Pond**, to your right, drains into **Burton Mill Pond**, on your left, and the marshland around it.

The view across to Chingford Pond and the South Downs includes the manor house of Burton Park. Originally built in 1831 as a private residence for Henry Bassett, Burton Park served for many years as a girls' school – St Michael's. The mansion, like many others in West Sussex, has been converted into luxury housing.

3 Stay on the **Serpent Trail** as it turns left into woodland. Within a few paces, leave the Serpent Trail by turning left again along a permissive path. The permissive path takes you up through beautiful, mature, open woodland, which skirts the marshland and **Burton Mill Pond**. Initially, as the path follows the edge of the wood, you have heathland on your right, until the path meets and follows the fence line of a grass field, which may contain livestock. At this point, you can again see the South Downs in the distance. The marshland comes round to cross the path. A series of boardwalks will take you safely over it.

4 At the end of the boardwalks, stay on the permissive path. Go through a gate into an enclosure, then turn right, continuing through woodland and onto open heathland. As you leave the woods, bear left, passing a noticeboard, then bear left again up the hill and keep going uphill on the broad track. Cross over the heathland to pass through another gate into a second enclosure. Head up the hill, but before you reach the top, turn right through a third gate onto a road.

5 You will now be at a road junction. If you look straight ahead, you can see a sign for a footpath by a gate. Cross here, and walk through the kissing gate. Turn left, and follow the marked footpath across a large grass field. Pass a ramshackle cow barn on your left. The path then bears left and slightly uphill towards a pylon. Climb the stile in front of the pylon, and turn left downhill. At the bottom of the hill, bear right to head back uphill towards another pylon.

6 At the pylon, pass through another kissing gate before following the fence line on your left down to a stile. This stile takes you onto the route of an old railway line. Very shortly, a third stile leads to a small paddock. Bear left, and head towards a large farm building. As you cross the paddock, you have views across the floodplain of the **River Rother**, towards **Fittleworth**. Just in front of the building, turn right towards the river, then turn left through a gate, which takes you up a short steep bank onto the road by **Shopham Bridge**.

(7) Turn left, away from the bridge, to walk along the quiet country lane. The road goes over a bridge crossing a disused railway line, shortly after which you cross the road to go through a kissing gate into a field on your right. Turn left, and follow the course of the road along the hedge line, towards woodland and parallel to the lane. (If there is livestock in the field, or it is muddy, you can choose to follow the lane down the field edge. At the end of

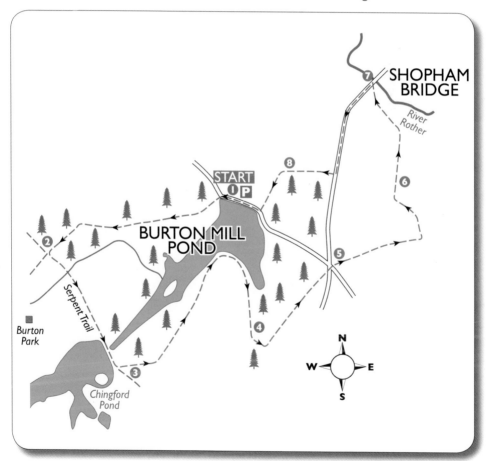

the field, cross a stile to rejoin the route at the woodland.) At the end of the field, negotiate the last stile, then turn right to follow the path between the woods and the field.

8 Follow the path, and turn left into the woods. Keep your dog close as the path drops downhill; very shortly, it meets the road opposite **Burton Mill Pond**. Turn right, and walk the short distance along the road beside the pond and back to the car park.

Looking over Burton Mill Pond to Grade I listed, Burton Park.

Flexham Park
2 miles (3.2 km)

Flexham Park in the spring.

Flexham Park is not a park but a privately owned, commercial, coppiced woodland with the Serpent Trail running through its middle. Either side of the trail is a network of forest tracks and paths which are open to the public. The very nature of a coppiced woodland means the route goes though areas of mature trees, young plantations and clearings. It also means that the views change depending on the growth or removal status of different areas of the woodland.

Coppicing is done on rotation: small areas of a woodland are cut each year in sequence, leaving the uncut areas to grow on for between 15 and 20 years for chestnut, and about 7 years for hazel. When an area of coppice is cut, it is all cut down, which creates a clearing.

The dogs love this short walk, as they can run free all the way around. Walkers will get to see the different stages of a coppiced wood, along with some lovely views across to the Surrey Hills.

How to get there & where to park

Approaching from the east, head towards Petworth on the Horsham Road (A272). Turn left onto Kingspit Lane, signed to Fittleworth. Take the left fork onto Riverhill Lane, and then turn left again onto a bridleway (a made road) where there is a parking area. **Sat nav** RH20 1JY.

OS map

Explorer OL34 Crawley & Horsham (GR TQ 001220).

Nearest refreshments

An inn since 1536, the Swan Inn at Fittleworth welcomes well-behaved dogs and has a lovely garden for sunny days. RH20 1EN.
☎ 01798 865154 www.theswanfittleworth.co.uk.

Dog factors

Terrain: Mainly easy going. A couple of steep inclines. Can be muddy in places after wet spells.
Road walking: None.
Livestock: None. Occasional horse riders.
Stiles: None.
Nearest vet: Newbridge Veterinary Surgery, Wharf Farm, Wisborough Green, RH14 0JG (on the A272) ☎ 01403 784777.

The Walk

1 From the car park, go through the metal gate onto the **Serpent Trail**, then immediately leave it by turning left. Follow the path along the edge of the woodland; in the winter, this can be wet in places. The path ends at a crossroads, with a fenced area in front of you. Go straight over the crossroads towards the fence line, then bear slightly right to follow it for just a few metres.

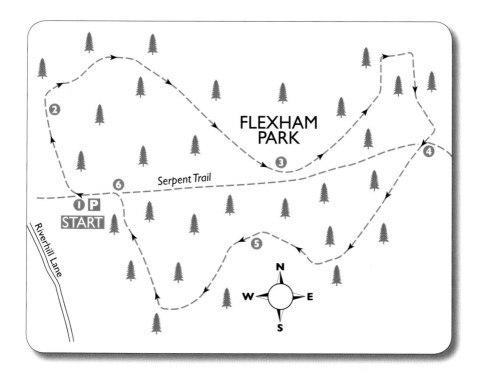

2 Take the first right to walk uphill into the woodland. The incline is quite steep but short. At the top of the hill, ignore the tracks on either side and keep straight ahead. Continue on this main track as it gently curves right, then goes fairly straight; when the path appears to divide, keep right. The track emerges from the woodland into a clearing, giving delightful views to your left towards the **Surrey Hills**. You will notice you are following the edge of the escarpment.

3 This track ends at a crossroads: to your left, the forest track goes downhill; and to your right is a fairly level, very wide track, edged by beautiful mature trees. Take the narrower path directly opposite to continue following the escarpment all the way around and up to the **Serpent Trail**. After a tight turn to the right, the path goes uphill. Towards the top of the hill keep right, still following the tree line until you get to a crossroads.

4 Cross over the wide path of the **Serpent Trail**, and take the path opposite, which starts to descend from the top of the hill. The path drops down, then curves a little way up again, turning into a hard forest track. There are various paths branching off the track, which should be ignored until the path joins another hard track coming downhill from your right.

5 At this point, keep straight ahead to join the descending path as it curves to the right. The hard track continues to run fairly straight, passing an enclosed area on your left. The track then curves around to the right, and the hard surface underfoot disappears. Continue to follow the wide track, ignoring narrower ones coming and going, until you reach another crossroads, where a hard track goes uphill to your right.

6 At this crossroads, turn left onto the hard track (the **Serpent Trail**); from here, you will shortly be in sight of the car park.

Petworth Park
3 miles (4.8 km)

Petworth House and Park.

Petworth House is the home of Lord Egremont and his family, who live in the south wing. The rest of the house is looked after by the National Trust and is open to the public. The 700-acre parkland, which is the setting for this walk, is one of the finest and most extensive remaining examples of landscaping by the famous Lancelot 'Capability' Brown, who designed it in 1750. There are two ponds which you will pass on the walk; Upper Pond, closest to the house, was designed to give the impression of a winding river rather than a formal pond.

For much of the walk, the tree planting and landscaping make it easy to believe you really are in open country rather than parkland surrounded by a high stone wall. The park is also home to around 500 fallow deer, one of the largest herds in the country, and as long as your dog is under control, you should be able to observe them at close quarters.

Dog factors

Terrain: The going is mainly good, on grass and hard tracks, but it can be a little wet underfoot in the winter. A couple of steep climbs.

Road walking: None.

Livestock: The whole walk is in a deer park, but the park is big enough to keep away from the deer for some off-lead walking. If your recall is still a 'work in progress', a long lead would be useful.

Stiles: None.

Nearest vet: Crofts Veterinary Practice, Collards Lane, Haslemere, GU27 2HU ☎ 01428 653056. If you park at New Lodge East, Midhurst is closer: Woodland Veterinary Centre, Grange Road, Midhurst, GU29 9LT ☎ 01730 814321.

How to get there & where to park

The National Trust car park at Petworth House is off the A283, 1½ miles north of Petworth. There is a charge if you are not a National Trust member. **Sat nav** GU28 9NN. Alternatively, there is limited parking by the gates at New Lodge East just off the Tillington Road (A272) between Petworth and Tillington. Go through the gates and straight up the track in front of you to the pond. You can pick up the walk at Point 4. **Sat nav** GU28 0QY.

OS map

Explorer OL33 Haslemere & Petersfield (GR SU 966238).

Nearest refreshments

The park is an ideal place for a picnic. Alternatively, the Stag Inn at Balls Cross serves good food and is dog-friendly. GU28 9JP ☎ 01403 820241. The Horse Guards Inn in Tillington is another favourite of mine. GU28 9AF ☎ 01798 342332.

The Walk

1 Heading south, leave the car park with the noticeboard to your right and the park wall to your left. Very soon, the path divides. Ignore the path that continues close to the wall, and take the one over to your right, which initially runs in the same direction. Follow this broad grass track, keeping an eye out for the deer herd. Ignore the joining paths. To your left, you will see the

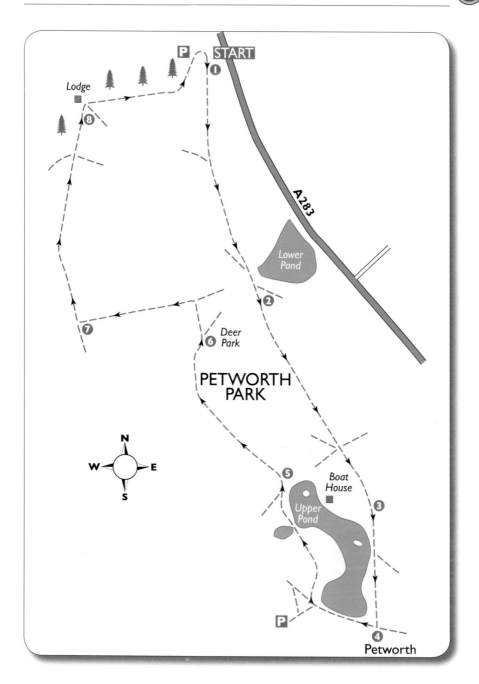

shimmer of water through the trees as you approach **Lower Pond**. Here, you veer slightly left to pick up the path alongside the pond.

2 As you approach the end of the pond, you will see a crossroad of tracks. Walk very slightly right onto the path that gradually climbs the hill in front of you. As you climb, look to the left and you will glimpse the kennels and the countryside beyond the park. Nearing the crest of the hill, you will see the South Downs in front of you. Ignore the track crossing the path near the top of the hill, and continue straight ahead until the path splits near a solar panel behind a small wooden fence.

3 At the solar panel, take the right fork, which soon starts to go downhill towards **Upper Pond**.

If, like mine, your dogs are more interested in birds than deer, it would be prudent to bring them in close, as the pond is a haven for water fowl.

Dropping down to walk alongside the pond, glance left to see the house start to appear around the side of the hill. You will get a full view as you cross the lawn between the house and the pond.

④ Having crossed the lawn, turn right onto the hard track. Follow this to the other side of the pond.

*If you parked at **New Lodge East**, this is where you join the route.*

Turn right onto a grass track, and follow this around the edge of the pond. Keeping the water on your right, follow the course of the track as it winds across the park. Look out for the boathouse on the far bank. You will lose sight of the water when you get to some iron railings. Follow the railings until they turn right.

⑤ The path you are on bends the same way as the rails; leave it to take the slightly narrower path straight ahead. This path is fairly straight until it bears right around the base of a hill.

⑥ Soon after this curve, with mature trees in front of you, take a short path to your left. Then turn left again at the T-junction. Follow this path uphill until it meets a hard track.

⑦ At the hard track, thankfully we don't take the very steep path ahead; instead, turn right to follow the fairly level hard track. Follow this track until you can see the **Lodge** (a house) and the park wall in front of you.

⑧ Turn right just before the **Lodge**. You are now on the homeward stretch. This path will take you back to the **National Trust car park**.

Heyshott
2 or 4 miles (3.2 or 6.4 km)

A run through Heyshott Common.

Heyshott Common is teeming with footpaths and bridleways and is crossed by two long-distance paths. It is open-access land, owned in the main by the Cowdray Estate and managed by the Wildlife Trust and Heathlands Reunited. It is an important part of a conservation plan to maintain and increase the small amount of heathland habitat within the South Downs National Park.

This figure-of-eight route starts on the heathland of Heyshott Common, where the colours and views are worth returning to see in every season. The walk crosses arable farmland, with views of the South Downs, and touches the edge of Heyshott village, with its popular pub, attractive pond and cricket pitch.

How to get there & where to park

From the A286 Cocking–Midhurst road, take the turning to Heyshott and Graffham. Stay on this road until the second crossroads. Turn left towards Ambersham onto New Road. Heyshott Common car park is on the left about ¼ mile from the crossroads. It is the only visible one on the left-hand side. **Sat nav** GU29 0BZ.

OS map

Explorers OL8 Chichester and OL10 Arundel & Pulborough (GR SU 912194).

Nearest refreshments

The Unicorn Inn at Heyshott is a short detour halfway around the route or a 5-minute drive from the car park. GU29 0DL
☎ 01730 813486 www.unicorn-inn-heyshott.co.uk.
The Greyhound, on the Cocking Causeway, is also dog-friendly. GU29 9QH
☎ 01730 814425 www.thegreyhoundpub.com.

Dog factors

Terrain: Mainly easy going, with a few moderate ascents. Paths can be wet underfoot in places, but are mostly sandy tracks.
Road walking: Two road crossings, with around 100 metres on a country lane at the first.
Livestock: None, but you may meet horse riders on the common. Between the end of March and July, you are asked to keep dogs to the paths due to ground-nesting birds.
Stiles: None. There are a couple of footbridges over small ditches; most dogs that don't like the bridges have no problem getting wet feet.
Nearest vet: Woodland Veterinary Centre, Grange Road, Midhurst, GU29 9LT ☎ 01730 814321.

The South Downs – A Dog Walker's Guide

The Walk
. . . .

1 From the back of the car park, ignore the wide track behind the noticeboard, and take the smaller one to the left. Where the path splits, take either path – they rejoin towards the bottom of the hill. Just after the paths reunite, ignore the small tracks to the right, and follow the path straight ahead for a few paces; then bear around to the left. The path takes you across the heathland through small pockets of trees. Keep bearing right until you come to a very sandy bridleway.

2 Turn right onto the bridleway, which will meet the **Serpent Trail** long-distance path. Continue straight ahead along the **Serpent Trail**.

If you have a mud-loving dog, it may find the 'wallow' just off this path. Luckily, if your dog does turn into a swamp monster, the path crosses a river a little further on, with easy dog access.

3 Soon after the river, turn left to leave the **Serpent Trail**. This path can start off muddy, as it is crossed by a clay belt before it returns to being a sandy path. The path bears round to the right before dividing. Ignore the right fork that goes up the steep hill, and bear left instead, following the path through the woods to the T-junction at the top.

4 Turn right at the top of the woodland path, then turn left uphill on a wider path. There is a little climb before you turn right onto a bridleway at a signpost. This bridleway will take you to another signpost at a major junction of paths.

If you have decided on the shorter route, turn right at this point, and follow the directions from Point 9.

5 On the longer route, you need to turn left to join the **New Lipchis Way**. The path goes between the trees, then across open heathland, giving a lovely view towards the **South Downs**. Back into the woods, there is a fairly steep descent, taking you to the road. Cross the road and turn right. Very shortly, you'll find the footpath on the left. Take the path straight ahead across the field, and climb towards the tree line to your left. Soon, you will start to get a view of **Heyshott** village, with a backdrop of the South Downs.

6 At the signpost, ignore the stile, and instead cross the footbridge slightly to your left. Follow a ditch and a hedge line on your right, and cross two more small bridges into a little copse before emerging in a large field. Turn left. You are now very close to the back of the village. The path takes you diagonally across to the signpost at the hedge on the other side of the field.

*If you fancy a break, a short detour here will take you to the **Unicorn Inn**. At the signpost, turn left, away from the route. When you get to the road, turn left again, and in a few paces the pub will be in sight.*

⑦ If you are continuing with the walk, turn right at the signpost. Keep the hedge line on your left to follow the footpath as it goes down the field, and turn left

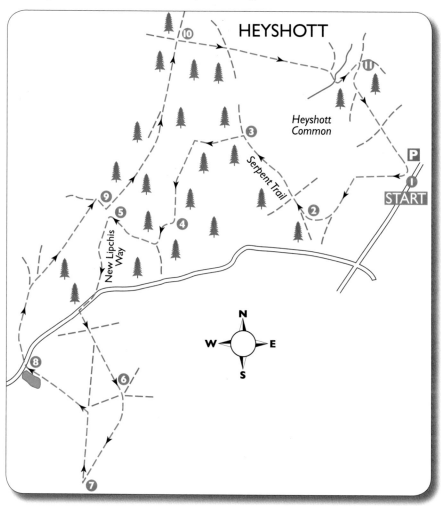

at the next signpost. Follow the field boundary round to the right, then keep left to leave this field over a ditch. Keep following the track towards a pylon. As you enter the next large field, turn left towards the pond. Keep the pond on your left, and you will soon arrive at a road opposite the village cricket pitch.

8 Cross the road on a slight diagonal, and follow the hard track around to the right, past the cricket pitch and a few cottages. Follow the footpath signs past the last cottages. Here, there is a short, steep climb back onto the heathland of the common. The narrow path wiggles through the heathland until it meets a wider, sandy path, where you turn right back to the crossroads at Point 5.

9 Turn left to follow a wide, sandy path. When it divides, bear left uphill. At the top of the hill, go slightly diagonally left across a flat, sandy area, then turn right along the track into the woods.

10 At the end of the woodland track, you will emerge onto a very wide, sandy crossroads. Turn right to follow the line of the overhead power cables.

The wide paths the power cables stand on are known as 'fire breaks'. There are usually small ponds at various points down this fire break, making it a favourite for my water-loving hounds.

At the bottom of the fire break, turn right down the bridleway, and cross the river over a wooden bridge; then turn left towards a couple of cottages.

11 Just after the garage on the right, turn right. The footpath goes up a few steps, and soon bears left onto the continuation of the fire break you left a few minutes ago. Very shortly, you will see the car park at the other end of the fire break.

Goodwood Country Park
4 miles (6.4 km)

Lovely view crossing Pilley Green field at Point 1.

Goodwood **Country Park is an area** to the south and east of the famous racecourse. In 1992, the Duke of Richmond granted a permissive right to allow members of the public to enjoy and walk in the country park. Our walk starts at Counters Gate, to the east of the racecourse, with a stroll through mature woodland. From here, the route is a mix of grass, arable, woodland and in places the route runs close to the road giving the dogs a rest as we keep them close. The extensive views across the racecourse, as well as the area surrounding Chichester are a highlight.

The South Downs – A Dog Walker's Guide

The varied woodland is a delightful mosaic of light and shade, and the dogs will get plenty of opportunity to stretch their legs. The path is near to the road, so keep them close and let them have a good sniff about.

How to get there & where to park

From the A286 at Singleton, turn onto Town Lane past the Weald & Downland Living Museum. At Goodwood Racecourse, turn left along Selhurstpark Road. There are a number of car parks opposite the racecourse on this road, but the one you want is Counters Gate car park, which is on the right after the end of the racecourse, and is named at the entrance. **Sat nav** PO18 0QE.

OS map

Explorer OL10 Arundel & Pulborough (GR SU 898113).

Nearest refreshments

If you don't fancy a picnic, the Fox Goes Free at Charlton is well worth a visit. PO18 0HU ☎ 01243 811461 www.thefoxgoesfree.com.

Dog factors

Terrain: Mostly good forest tracks, with a little grassland and one long, fairly gentle incline.

Road walking: Four crossings, but all quiet country roads. A few metres of road walking at the third crossing. A couple of the paths do run alongside these roads.

Livestock: There may be sheep in the first field we cross and in the well-fenced field straight after that.

Stiles: None.

Nearest vet: Mark Elliott and Associates, Madam Green Business Centre, High Street, Oving, West Sussex, PO20 2DD ☎ 01243 779111.

The Walk

1 From **Counters Gate car park**, look for a gap in the bank behind the parking area where a footpath crosses the grass into woodland. Once you are in the woodland, turn left onto a well-made-up path. Continue along the footpath to the wooden gate into **Pilley Green field**. Follow the field path to the right-hand corner, joining **Eastdean Hill Road**.

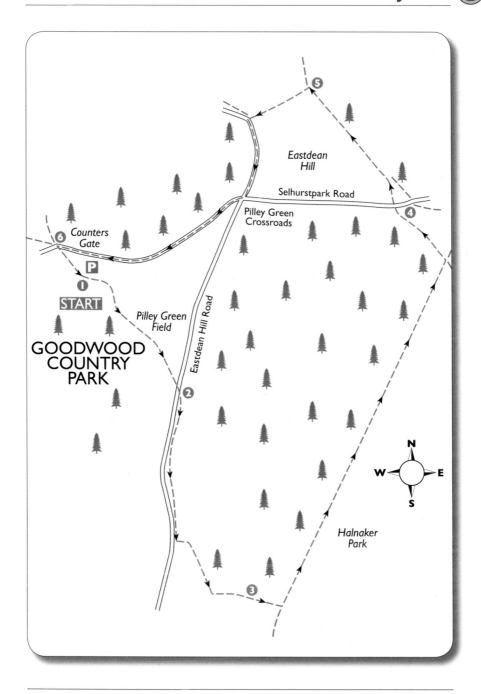

⑤

Eastdean Hill

Selhurstpark Road

Pilley Green
Crossroads

④

⑥ *Counters Gate*

Ⓟ

① START

Pilley Green Field

Eastdean Hill Road

GOODWOOD COUNTRY PARK

②

N
W · E
S

Halnaker Park

③

2 At the road, cross over through the wooden footpath gate, and walk down the side of the field, keeping the hedge on your right. You will see **Halnaker Windmill** in the distance on your left. At the end of the field, follow the footpath to the left, then right, down the gravel track. The track leads down the hill into woodland. Turning left when it meets a field, follow the field line towards **Halnaker Park**.

3 At the signpost, turn left onto a small track through the trees. When this track reaches a wider track, turn left again to stay on the bridleway. This long, straight track gradually climbs up to a signpost; here, you swing left then right to keep following the track to a metal gate onto **Selhurstpark Road**.

4 Cross the road to join the footpath across the corner of the field and through the wood, bearing left into the wood. At the next cross-paths, turn left back towards the field.

5 Following the footpath across the field on **Eastdean Hill**, take a moment to admire the view. Turn left along the hedge line, keeping the hedge on your right to emerge on **Eastdean Hill Road** just below **Pilley Green crossroads**. Cross the road and turn left, passing the first footpath, heading towards the crossroads. Just before the crossroads, at the bridleway, turn right through the trees.

6 Turn left at the end of the bridleway, and cross the road, joining the footpath on the opposite side of the road; this will take you back into **Counters Gate car park**.

Woolbeding Parkland
3¾ miles (6 km)

The grass parkland at Woolbeding.

This is a lovely walk close to the busy town of Midhurst, which lies in the heart of the South Downs National Park. The walk starts on the National Trust-owned Woolbeding Estate, part of the Rother Valley, and is mainly over grass parkland and arable land. There are spectacular views of the Rother Valley, a folly to explore, some woodland and an old drovers' trail. You'll get a glimpse of Woolbeding House, the home of the late Simon Sainsbury of the Sainsbury's supermarket family, who sold the estate to the National Trust in the 1950s but remained living there until his death in 2006. The final part of the walk takes in the marshes by the River Rother, shaded by ancient oak trees, before returning to the parkland.

The South Downs – A Dog Walker's Guide

How to get there & where to park
The Woolbeding Estate is a mile west of Midhurst. From Midhurst, take the A272 towards Petersfield. Just past the Half Moon pub, turn right for Woolbeding, and park in the National Trust car park on your right. **Sat nav** GU29 9RR.

OS map
Explorer OL33 Haslemere & Petersfield (GR SU 872227).

Nearest refreshments
Midhurst is a pretty town and worth a visit. Fitzcane's café in North Street is very close to the car park and dog-friendly inside and out. In the opposite direction, the Glasshouse Café at Rotherhill Nurseries in Stedham is very welcoming to dogs, and the home-cooked food is always good.

Dog factors
Terrain: Mainly easy walking, with some moderate inclines.
Road walking: None.
Livestock: The National Trust has a small herd of cows and sheep which may be in the parkland at the beginning and end of the walk. Take note of any signs on the gate in the car park; the National Trust usually lets walkers know when there is livestock in the fields.
Stiles: None.
Nearest vet: Woodland Veterinary Centre, Grange Road, Midhurst, GU29 9LT ☎ 01730 814321.

The Walk

1 From the car park, go through the kissing gate into the parkland. Following the main track running from the large gate, go straight across two fields of open grassland. In the second field, you will get your first view of **Woolbeding House** to your right, and the **South Downs**. A little further up the hill, the view includes the **River Rother**, Woolbeding's lovely church and a lake. At the top of the field, go through a kissing gate into **Whiphill Wood**. The wood ends at another gate into a field. Here you will have a good view of a Grade II listed former rectory, **Glebe House**. The route takes you diagonally right and downhill, with a folly to your right.

This is open-access land, so it's fine to take a slight detour to view the folly.

In the bottom right-hand corner of the field, we leave National Trust land through another kissing gate.

② Follow the signs for the **'River Walk'**. The river is unseen below you to your left. Stay with the river walk as it tracks fairly straight along the bottom of an arable field and on into another.

③ Going under some power lines, pass the end of a hedgerow into the second field. After a few metres, the river walk leaves you as it turns left; you continue straight ahead. Keep the tree and hedge line on your left, and follow the field boundary straight ahead. The track continues to follow the tree line slightly uphill to join the track coming out of a small wood to your left.

The going underfoot is usually good, but the trees to your left often hide the marshland by the river from view. This means adventurous dogs may get rather mucky.

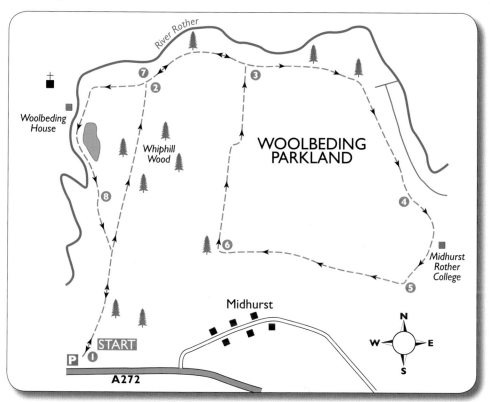

4 Turn left to follow the path uphill through the wood as it bears right along a drovers' trail before emerging at the back gates to **Midhurst Rother College**.

5 Turn right into an open field, then turn immediately left to follow the permissive path as it follows along the tree line. Behind the tree line are horse paddocks. When the permissive path turns left, continue straight ahead on the farm track with the fence line on your right. When the fence ends, continue straight across the field to join a wide track below the power lines.

6 Enjoy the view of the Downs as you turn right to follow the power lines downhill. At the field junction, do a dog-leg to go fairly straight while keeping the pylons and hedge on your left. This will bring you back to your outward route at Point 3. Turn left to retrace your steps back to the National Trust Woolbeding Estate at Point 2.

*You now have the choice either to retrace your route back through **Whiphill Wood** to the car park, or to go back via the marshland beside the river.*

7 To return via the river: after the kissing gate, follow the fence line at the bottom of the field to another gate. Go through this gate into the marshland. The path can be difficult to see when the ground is wet. It goes straight towards the house and river before turning left by a few trees. As long as you keep the river on your right, you can't go far wrong. Following the course of the river past the lake, the path is again easy to follow to a 5-bar gate with a kissing gate to the left.

8 Follow the vehicle tracks from the 5-bar gate diagonally left, uphill out of the marsh. The tracks follow the brow of the hill before bearing left onto the route of your outward journey. Turn right, back into the field you started your walk in, and the car park will soon be in sight.

Stoughton Down to the Devil's Humps

4½ miles (7.2 km)

The Devil's Humps.

This route takes you along woodland paths, grass rides and stony tracks, with fantastic views for half the walk. The woods are a delightful mixture of beech, oak and yew trees. Kingley Vale is thought to be one of Europe's most extensive ancient yew forests; yews have been on this site for many hundreds of years, and some of the trees are thought to be more than 2,000 years old.

The walk also takes you past the Devil's Humps, a series of four Bronze Age barrows or burial mounds. The alternative name for the mounds is Kings' Graves, a name from folklore that suggests Viking leaders were buried here after they were defeated by the men of Chichester. It is the extensive views from this point, along with the ancient yew trees, that earn Kingley Vale National Nature Reserve the nickname 'Yews and Views'.

Dog factors

Terrain: Mostly wide, forest grass tracks and hard tracks, but it can be muddy under the trees. One long climb and an equivalent descent.
Road walking: None, but you may meet the odd forestry or wardens' vehicle en route.
Livestock: The occasional horse and rider. There may be sheep at the Devil's Humps.
Stiles: None.
Nearest vet: Horndean Veterinary Surgery, St Peter's Vets Ltd, 67 Portsmouth Road, Horndean, Waterlooville, PO8 9LH
☎ 02392 592526.

How to get there & where to park

The Stoughton Down Forestry Commission car park can be found on a sharp bend on the road midway between the small villages of Stoughton and East Marden in West Sussex. **Sat nav** PO18 9JG.

OS map

Explorer OL8 Chichester (GR SU 815126).

Nearest refreshments

The Hare & Hounds in Stoughton is privately owned and has been a focal point of village life since the 19th century. Dogs, children and walkers are all made very welcome. PO18 9JQ ☎ 02392 631433 www.hareandhoundspub.co.uk. Alternatively, take a picnic to enjoy at the Humps or on the grass bank of the car park.

The Walk

1 From the car park, join the wide, stone track beyond the metal vehicle barrier. Follow this track, with woodland to your right and an open field to your left. At the fork, keep left to leave the main stony track, and follow the bridleway into the woodland. When this bridleway bears left at another fork, keep straight ahead to follow the uphill path. Keep climbing as the path curves left. Continue climbing as you pass the boundary fence for **Blackbush House** on your left, just before you reach a junction.

Stoughton Down to the Devil's Humps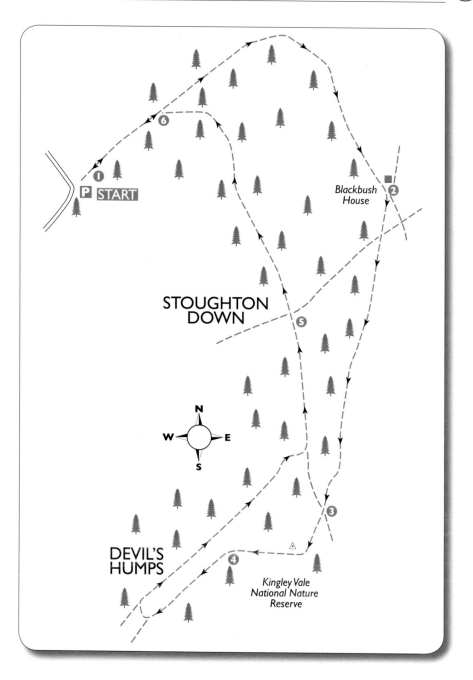

The South Downs – A Dog Walker's Guide

Now a large family home, Blackbush House was built in the 18th century by the groom to the bedchamber of George II, as a smallpox isolation hospital. It featured on the BBC's The House Detectives.

② The path meets the bridleway that goes past the front of the property. However, you will need to turn right, away from the house. You are now on a broad grass ride that follows the ridge of the **Downs**. Stay on this bridleway, going straight on when a couple of other bridleways cross your path.

③ When you get to the junction by the **Kingley Vale National Nature Reserve** sign, continue, following the bridleway straight on. Soon you'll start following a fence line to your left. A trig point to your right marks the top of **Bow Hill**.

④ Passing through a gateway, you get your first sight of the **Devil's Humps**.

Take time to enjoy the views from the top of the Devil's Humps. To the north, you'll have views further across the South Downs, with the suburbs of Portsmouth just visible over to the far left. It is the views to the south that really make the climb worthwhile. Chichester Cathedral's spire stands tall as an obvious landmark. On clear days, the sea will be visible, with the Isle of Wight across to the west and Bognor Regis to the east.

When you have finished exploring the **Devil's Humps**, pick up the bridleway on the opposite side to the one you arrived on. Turn right on the wide track, passing a **Kingley Vale** sign on your right. Stay on this bridleway, and descend to a junction of several paths. On your way down, you'll see views to the Downs on your left and ancient yew trees to your right.

⑤ At the junction, the hard track bears right, but you need to follow the bridleway straight ahead onto a delightful woodland path. This path takes you past beech and oak trees, gently curving as it continues to descend until it rejoins the hard track.

⑥ As you join the hard track, bear left to follow it back to the car park.

West Harting Down to Ladyholt

3½ miles (5.6 km)

Dogs can run free on the open forest paths.

West Harting Down is owned by the Forestry Commission, so it is a working forest. With no official car park (see below for where to park) it tends to be less busy than its neighbour, the National Trust-owned Harting Hill. Criss-crossed by public footpaths and bridleways, with open-access forestry roads and paths, West Harting Down allows your dogs to run free for most of the way.

The route starts on an uphill stretch on a forestry road, then follows woodland tracks through Eckensfield Farm and onto a hard, open track with extensive views, before dropping down towards Ladyholt. A woodland path then joins the Sussex Border Path as it winds its way back up to the top of the Downs, where wide forestry tracks take you back to the car park.

The South Downs – A Dog Walker's Guide

How to get there & where to park

There is room for a couple of cars to park on the wide road turning at the Forestry Commission gate to West Harting Down. The entrance is just off, and visible from, the B2146 between South Harting and Compton. From South Harting, you will find it on the right about a mile after Uppark House. **Sat nav** GU31 5QS.

OS map

Explorer OL8 Chichester (GR SU 773169).

Nearest refreshments

The Victoria Inn at West Marden is a traditional pub serving good food. Dogs are welcome in the bar and garden. PO18 9EN ☎ 02392 631330 www.victoriainnwestmarden.co.uk.

Dog factors

Terrain: Wide forestry tracks and winding woodland paths. The going can be wet in places, but is mainly good. Undulating with some long uphill stretches, rising to 453 feet in altitude at the highest point.
Road walking: Officially none, but you may come across vehicles on the forestry tracks and the hard track between Eckensfield Farm and Ladyholt.
Livestock: None, but horse riders are very likely, and deer live in the woods.
Stiles: None.
Nearest vet: Petersfield Veterinary Centre, St Peter's Vets Ltd, St Peter's Road, Petersfield, GU31 4AA ☎ 01730 266431.

The Walk

1 Having parked clear of the metal gate, walk past the **Forestry Commission** sign, and follow the hard track uphill until it is crossed by a footpath.

2 Turn left onto the footpath. Follow the footpath through the woods and straight over a major junction onto a bridleway. Follow the bridleway until it runs along the woodland boundary. Look left through the trees, and you will get a glimpse of the view across the fields. The sight of a building further

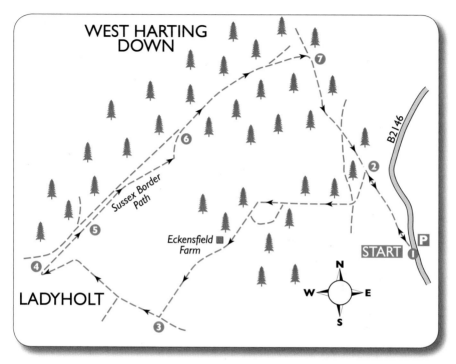

along the bridleway means you are approaching **Eckensfield Farm**. This is more of a private house with a stable yard than a farm, but they do have 'free range' dogs, so it would be prudent to keep yours close. Pass Eckensfield Farm, and leave the woodland for a while. Keep straight ahead past a few more houses, and soon you will arrive at a signpost on a T-junction.

❸ Turn right along the wide, stony path through an avenue of trees, and go gently uphill. At the brow of the hill, you can take in the extensive views across the arable land towards **Portsdown Hill** to your left. As the path begins to descend, you will see the trees of West Harting Down woodland ahead. As you reach the edge of the woodland, the track turns left towards the hamlet of **Ladyholt**.

❹ Just before you reach the hamlet, turn sharp right, almost back on yourself, into the woodland. You are now on a pleasant woodland path which runs fairly straight for a while. Look to your left, and you'll soon see a stony track a little below, and parallel to, the path you're on. Before long, your path turns left towards this and through a metal gate, but you will need to keep straight ahead instead.

5 Do not turn left towards the gate; instead, go straight ahead onto the **Sussex Border Path**, which is a narrow track into the woods. There is a round disc with an arrow on a tree stump on your right. At this point, the **Sussex Border Path** is a narrow track that winds its way gradually up to the top of the **Downs**. Fallen trees occasionally force a little detour, but on the whole the path is well-walked and easy to follow. If in doubt, remember it goes uphill. As you near the top of the **Downs**, the path runs close to an arable field. A signpost near the top will reassure you that you are still on the **Sussex Border Path**.

6 Very soon, you are out of the woods, and another signpost points right as the **Sussex Border Path** joins a wide forestry track. Stay on this fairly level track. Leave the **Sussex Border Path** when it turns left back into the woods, and continue on the wider forestry track until it meets a bridleway at a T-junction.

7 Turn right onto the bridleway, a wide forestry track. When it is crossed by another bridleway, stay on your path, the wider forestry track. Cross over the footpath at Point 2. Now retrace your steps for the final ¼ mile back to your car.

Older Hill and Woolbeding Common

5 miles (8 km)

The dogs enjoying the open heathland.

The South Downs – A Dog Walker's Guide

This varied walk starts in the National Trust car park at the top of Older Hill, on the edge of Woolbeding Common. Starting out on open heathland with views of the South Downs, the dogs will have plenty of room for a good romp. Dogs can run free for a good deal of this walk, but a lead will be needed at a couple of road crossings and, at one point, where there is free-range poultry. Open heathland, woodland tracks, grassy fields, a deep valley with gentle inclines and a couple of steep descents: this route has it all, and with the exception of the woodland, there are also plenty of great views.

Dog factors

Terrain: Fairly easy going, with a couple of steep downhill sections.
Road walking: A few road crossings and a couple of very short sections on country lanes. Some of the hard tracks do have limited vehicle access.
Livestock: You will pass fields with cows and sheep. Occasionally, the National Trust puts up temporary fencing to graze their cows on the common. Horses are possible on the bridleways.
Stiles: None.
Nearest vet: Woodland Veterinary Centre, Grange Road, Midhurst, GU29 9LT ☎ 01730 814321.

How to get there & where to park
Head for the free National Trust car park at the top of Older Hill. From Midhurst, take the A272 towards Petersfield. After the Half Moon pub, take the right turn signposted to Woolbeding. At the junction, turn left up the hill. Continue up the hill towards Redford for about a mile. Before you reach Redford, turn right up the lane at the Older Hill sign, and continue until you reach the car park. **Sat nav** GU29 9RR.

OS map
Explorer OL33 Haslemere & Petersfield (GR SU 869260).

Nearest refreshments
The viewpoint opposite the car park is the ideal place to have a picnic. Fitzcane's café on North Street in Midhurst and the Glasshouse Café at Rotherhill Nurseries in Stedham are both dog-friendly.

The Walk

1 Facing the noticeboard in the car park, turn right through the trees to cross a track. Take the path ahead onto the heathland, where you will start the gentle descent of **Older Hill**.

2 Soon, the **New Lipchis Way** (a long-distance path that runs for 39 miles from Liphook to Chichester) crosses the track. Turn right to stay on the **New Lipchis Way**. You will soon be under the trees, with fields to your left where there are often horses. Pass a wooden barrier, and continue to follow the footpath past a few properties on your left; then cross a lane. From here, the marked footpath down through the trees to the Redford road (**Linch Road**) is fairly steep.

3 At the bottom of the hill, take care as you cross the road into a small car park. At the back of the car park, turn left along a fence line to continue to follow the **New Lipchis Way** around the edge of **Stedham Marsh**. Passing a couple of signposts, keep going fairly straight ahead until you get to the fenced fields of **Woolhouse Farm**.

4 As the path turns to the left, there is a sign asking you to keep your dogs on a lead due to free-range birds. You are now on a farm track, which you follow past the buildings and fields until it runs into the tarmac end of Tote Lane. Follow the **New Lipchis Way** as it turns right off the lane to follow the fence line. The fields to your right usually house cattle, and sometimes sheep. Pass the parking area for a fishing club. You are now on a delightful woodland path that follows a ridge high above the river. When the **New Lipchis Way** turns right to go steeply downhill, you need to stay on the footpath along the upper ridge and follow it as it curves to the left to a junction with another footpath and a bridleway. Here, keep bearing left uphill until you are on a path running alongside a fenced field. Keep the fence line on your left to follow the footpath past a few cottages – and possibly more free-range chickens – to the junction with **Tote Lane**.

5 Turn left to briefly follow **Tote Lane**, then turn right across the lane onto a footpath. Follow the footpath past **Woodgate Farm** into an open field. Enjoy the views of the Downs as you cross the field to a small copse of trees. The track through the trees brings you back to the Redford road (**Linch Road**).

6 Cross the road, and turn right. Within a few metres, you reach the footpath sign directing you left off the road towards **Denne House**. Follow the footpath through a small car park and onto **Pound Common**. Take the hard track

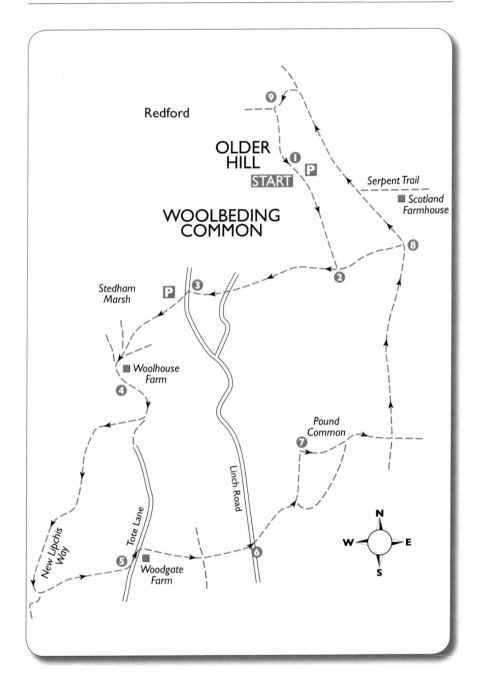

in front of you until you reach **Denne House** on the right. Leave the footpath, and turn left up the grassy valley.

7 At the crossroads at the top of the valley, turn right, where a short, steeper incline brings you to a level track with views across to the **South Downs**. Follow this track, ignoring the track coming up from your right. Stay on the footpath as it gently curves along a tree line at the bottom of a large area of open heathland. At the next signpost, turn left uphill to follow the footpath across the heathland. When the footpath turns right into a small wooded area, stay on the track that goes straight ahead alongside the wood, emerging in a small car park at the top of the hill.

8 Going diagonally across the car park, turn left onto a hard track. Although not a road, this is the access route for a couple of houses and a stable yard, so vehicles do use it. As you pass the drive for **Scotland Farmhouse**, the **Serpent Trail** joins your track, but not for long. When the **Serpent Trail** turns left downhill, keep straight ahead. Just before the hard track ends, turn left downhill on a narrow track through the trees. At the next signpost, bear slightly left to continue on the narrow, steep, downhill path. Take care, as the going is very uneven and can be slippery. The path ends on a little lane; again, this is just a drive to a few houses, but vehicles do use it.

9 Cross the lane to a wooden bench, where you will be treated to panoramic views across **Redford** to the **Downs** and beyond. Turn left in front of the bench, and continue to enjoy the views as you follow the narrow, winding path back to the viewpoint opposite the car park.

Black Down
2 or 3½ miles (3.2 or 5.6 km)

Having a rest at the Temple of the Winds.

Black **Down was once owned by** Alfred, Lord Tennyson. Tiring of the summer tourists around his home on the Isle of Wight, the poet had Aldworth House built on the Black Down Estate so he could find peace in the summer months. He died there in October 1892.

Despite being privately owned by various people over the years, Black Down has always been common grazing land, which has maintained it as a heathland. With the decline of its use for grazing, trees thrived and the wooded areas increased. In 1944, Black Down was given to the National Trust, who have fenced the area and are using a programme of logging and grazing to maintain the heathland.

This delightful walk is on mainly sandy paths across heathland and through wooded areas. One lovely track is named Pen-y-bos, which is Celtic in origin, giving a clue to the historic importance of the area. Throughout the walk you are treated to lovely views of Hampshire, Surrey and West Sussex across to the South Downs. As long as they don't bother the cows, the dogs can run free all the time you are in the enclosure.

Dog factors

Terrain: Moderate walking, with one long, steep climb. Mainly level sand paths. The shorter route avoids the long climb.
Road walking: None, apart from a few metres along an access road at the end of the walk. The entire walk is within the fenced area of Black Down heathland.
Livestock: A small herd of Belted Galloway cattle graze Black Down. Horse riders use the bridleways.
Stiles: None.
Nearest vet: Crofts Veterinary Practice, Collards Lane, Haslemere, GU27 2HU ☎ 01428 653056.

How to get there & where to park
From Haslemere, take the B2131 Petworth Road, then turn right up Haste Hill, which leads to Tennyson's Lane. The walk starts at the back of the National Trust Black Down car park off Tennyson's Lane. **Sat nav** GU27 3BJ.

OS map
Explorer OL33 Haslemere & Petersfield (GR SU 921309).

Nearest refreshments
There are lots of lovely places on the route to stop if you have packed your own picnic. If not, the Red Lion, a few miles away at Fernhurst, is dog-friendly. ☎ 01428 643112 www.red-lion-fernhurst.co.uk. Haslemere does have a few dog-friendly pubs, but the traffic and parking can be difficult.

The Walk

1 From the car park, take the track opposite the entry from **Tennyson's Lane**. Bear right, and then walk through the gate into the **Black Down** enclosure. Follow the narrow path through the trees; it runs slightly downhill and bears left until it joins a slightly wider track. Turn left. Now you are on the ancient **Pen-y-bos path**. Staying on this path, keep slightly right when it splits. When the path merges with a wide, lower bridleway, bear very slightly right to join it. Very shortly you will come to a junction of paths.

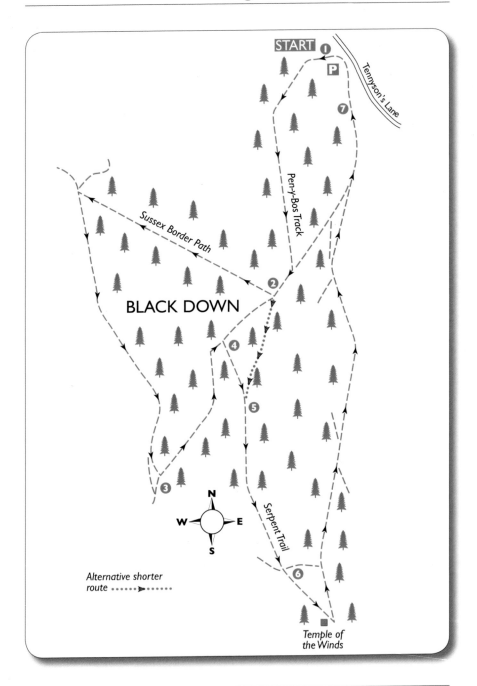

START ❶

P

Tennyson's Lane

❼

Pen-y-Bos Track

Sussex Border Path

❷

BLACK DOWN

❹

❺

❸

N
W   E
S

Serpent Trail

❻

Alternative shorter
route ••••••▶••••••

Temple of
the Winds

*For the shorter, easier route, go straight ahead on the same path (the **Serpent Trail**) at the junction, and continue until you get to a bench and a viewpoint with a map on a pedestal. Then follow directions from Point 5.*

2 At the junction, the shorter route goes straight ahead, but the longer route turns right and follows the bridleway along the route of the **Sussex Border Path**. Here, you will be treated to your first glimpse of the extensive views this route has to offer. When the track divides, keep left to follow the **Sussex Border Path** downhill to the bottom of the enclosure. At the bottom of the track, ignore the gate in front of you and turn left. Leaving the Sussex Border Path, follow a lovely wide bridleway through the trees.

3 This lower path again ends in a gate that you ignore. Instead, turn hard left, away from the gate, to start the steep climb back up the bridleway to the heathland. As you near the top, the trees that have lined your route start to disappear. The path is joined by a number of small paths; these should be ignored, but they give an indication that you are nearing the top.

4 Just before the brow of the hill, turn right at a crossroads. Follow the track to a viewpoint to take in the spectacular views. Here, there is a bench and a map on a pedestal, making it an ideal spot for a breather or a picnic.

5 At this point, the track joins the wider path of the **Serpent Trail**, a rambling, 64-mile long-distance path from Haslemere to Petersfield. From the bench, bear right. Except for a short detour to take in the **Temple of the Winds**, you will now stay with the **Serpent Trail** to the end of your journey. The going underfoot is now fairly level, and the path is wide, with a few gentle bends. The path climbs a short hill to bring you nearly to the top of **Black Down**, at 280 metres. Just after the path becomes wooded and levels again, look for the **Temple of the Winds** sign to your right, just before a signpost.

6 Turn right to take a short detour from the Serpent Trail to visit the Temple. This is a panoramic viewpoint across to the **South Downs**. Using the map on a pedestal, it's easy to pick out landmarks in the distance. Alternatively, you can take a seat on the stone bench memorial and enjoy the peaceful setting. Then retrace your steps back towards the signpost, bearing right at the fork, then right again, to rejoin the **Serpent Trail**. Now follow the signs for the Serpent Trail through the wood and heathland; there are plenty of water splashes en route for the dogs. Shortly after passing the **Black Down** noticeboard, you arrive at a gate.

7 Go through the gate, and follow the hard track past a small car park. Turn left just before the track meets **Tennyson's Lane**, and return to the car park.

Chapel Common to Foley Manor
5½ miles (8.9 km)

Chapel Common.

Chapel **Common is a** Site of Special Scientific Interest, so this is a suitably varied walk through woods, across heathland and near to the manicured grounds of Liphook Golf Club. The dogs will need to be kept close or on leads in places, but they will have plenty of opportunity to run free for most of the walk. The route mainly follows the long-distance paths of the Serpent Trail, the Sussex Border Path and the Shipwrights Way. It crosses Chapel Common, then passes an old farmyard and onto the golf course. A woodland path takes you around the back of Forest Mere, health spa to the rich and famous, before a stroll alongside Folly Pond and onto the Sussex Border Path under the railway line returns you to Chapel Common.

How to get there & where to park

From the B2070, travelling from Liphook towards Rake, turn right down the lane alongside Rake Primary School. The next right is an unmade road with a sign at the end warning of the uneven surface. Chapel Common is at the end of this lane; park where you can find a spot on the lane, or on the similar one that runs in front of the enclosure. **Sat nav** GU33 7JL.

OS map

Explorer OL33 Haslemere & Petersfield (GR SU 814286).

Nearest refreshments

The Black Fox Inn, on Portsmouth Road in Liphook, is dog-friendly and serves good food. GU30 7JJ ☎ 01428 723218.

Dog factors

Terrain: Easy going: mainly sandy or woodland tracks, and no serious hills.

Road walking: Approximately 20 metres on the grass verge alongside a fairly busy road; ¾ mile on a tarmac private drive at the Foley Estate.

Livestock: The National Trust's docile Belted Galloway cattle may be on Chapel Common. There are lots of bridleways, so keep an eye out for horses.

Stiles: None.

Nearest vet: Liss Veterinary Surgery, St Peter's Vets Ltd, Mill Road, Liss, Hampshire, GU33 7AZ ☎ 01730 894222.

The Walk

1 Having parked along the unmade lane, make your way to the main gate into **Chapel Common**. It's easy to spot: there is a large, wooden sign near the gate, and a noticeboard a few metres to the right of the gate. Bearing slightly right through the gate, pick up the **Serpent Trail** to go through the trees ahead. The tree-lined path continues fairly straight ahead, with glimpses of heathland and lots of joining and crossing paths. The dogs may want to stop for a splash in the small pond you pass on your right. Continue straight ahead until you come out onto open heathland.

2 Almost as soon as you leave the trees, you come to a signpost, where you turn left to continue on the **Serpent Trail**, bearing slightly right over open heathland. After a short climb, the **Serpent Trail** turns left along a ridge into another tree-lined path. Cross a bridleway, and another signpost directs you slightly downhill along the **Serpent Trail** to the gate out of the **Chapel Common** enclosure. Staying on the **Serpent Trail**, a fairly straight path takes you towards the railway line and another signpost.

3 At this signpost, leave the Serpent Trail, and turn right along the bridleway towards the farm buildings of **Ripsley Farm**. Walk diagonally across a small paddock, then through the farmyard, and follow a hard track onto the golf course, taking care to look out for flying golf balls. The hard track will take you to the road.

4 At the road, turn left along the grass verge. It is a busy road, but you are not on it for long. Look for the turning on the left about 20 metres in front of you. This left turn takes you back onto the golf course, down a tarmac drive. Follow the drive over the railway bridge.

5 As soon as you are over the bridge, cross diagonally right over the drive onto a tree-lined path. This path bears around to the right to join a bridleway. Follow the bridleway straight ahead, ignoring a footpath off to the right. The path runs between trees lining the golf course to your right and fields to your left. You'll emerge onto a hard track, where you bear slightly left; then continue up the hard track until it meets the **Shipwrights Way** on its journey from Alice Holts to Portsmouth.

6 Turn left to follow the **Shipwrights Way** down the tarmac drive of the **Foley Estate**. This is a pleasant, tree-lined drive with a pretty pond to the left. Around a gentle bend, you are greeted by the fine statue of Lord Strathnairn.

Lord Strathnairn (1801–1885) was a senior British Army officer and Commander-in-Chief of the army in India and then in Ireland.

Turn right with the **Shipwrights Way**, continuing down the **Foley Estate** drive past the lakes on your right. When the path splits, turn right towards **Keepers Cottage**. Pass Keepers Cottage, and keep going straight ahead until the tarmac drive runs onto a rough track.

7 Almost as soon as you reach the rough track, leave the **Shipwrights Way**, and turn left down the bridleway which runs through the wood, giving the dogs a chance to stretch their legs again. For most of the way through this wood, you are following the fence line on your left as it runs around the back of the **Foley Estate** to join the boundary with the **Forest Mere Estate**. Keeping

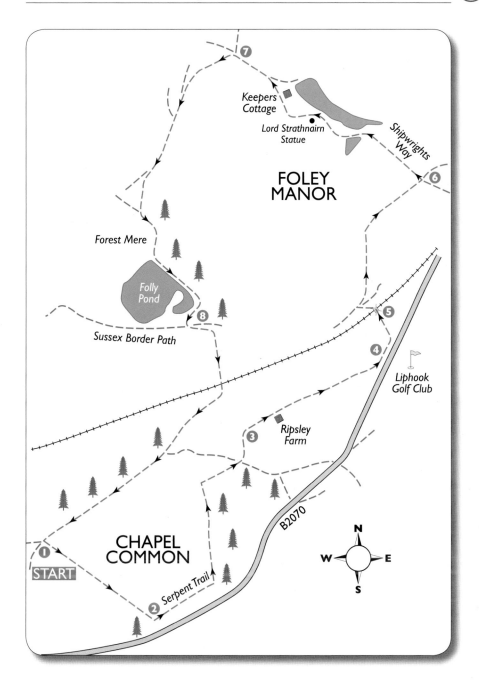

left at the bridleway junctions, pass the grounds of **Forest Mere** – you can glimpse the health spa to your right – before joining the drive. The bridleway follows the tarmac drive to just past **Folly Pond**, then bears right through the trees. At the end of the trees, the bridleway turns right towards **Home Farm**, meeting the **Sussex Border Path** just before the brick pillars.

8 Here, turn left onto the **Sussex Border Path**. At the next signpost, turn right to stay on the **Sussex Border Path** as it makes its way under the railway line. Having passed under the bridge, leave the long-distance path, and turn right down the bridleway, with the railway line to your right. The bridleway and railway line gradually move away from each other, and soon you are again in sight of the gates to **Chapel Common**. The bridleway bears right through the lower of the two visible gates. This route across the common is wooded. The first half has a higher and a lower path running alongside each other; the lower one can be wet underfoot. These paths take you across the enclosure to another gate. After you have passed through this gate, follow the enclosure boundary fence back to the parking area.

Folly Pond.

Steep to Ashford Hangers
4 miles (6.4 km)

Enjoying the view on the Hangers Way just before the Poet's Stone.

Starting in the village of Steep, this walk goes through woodland and crosses fields up into the Ashford Hangers National Nature Reserve, one of Hampshire's most beautiful woodland areas. The poet Edward Thomas and his wife, Helen, lived here before his death in the First World War; the poet mentions the hillside in many of his poems, and on the route you will pass a memorial stone, the Poet's Stone, dedicated to him. The area consists of 323 acres of woodland and beech hanger, with magnificent views over the surrounding area. The word 'hanger' comes from the Old English *hangra*, meaning a wooded slope.

How to get there & where to park
Steep is 2 miles north of Petersfield. Head for All Saints Church in the centre of the village, where there is some parking along Church Road. **Sat nav** GU32 2DF.

The South Downs – A Dog Walker's Guide

OS map
Explorer OL33 Haslemere & Petersfield (GR SU 745253).

Nearest refreshments
If you take a picnic, there are plenty of nice places to stop and enjoy it on the route. A couple of miles away, the Harrow Inn serves good food and real ale. Dogs are welcome inside and out, but as both bars are legally classed as such, and not as restaurants, children can only enjoy the garden. GU32 2DU ☎ 01730 262685 www.harrow-inn.co.uk.

Dog factors
Terrain: Underfoot, a mix of woodland paths, semi-hard tracks and grassland. It is very steep up and down, in places. Luckily there are easier sections in between for recovery.
Road walking: A couple of short road sections, in total around ½ mile.
Livestock: Likely on the way out, between Points 2 and 5. There may also be sheep in the enclosure of Wheatham Hill, which is passed en route.
Stiles: Three, all easily negotiated by my large Labradors.
Nearest vet: Petersfield Veterinary Centre, St Peter's Vets Ltd, St Peter's Road, Petersfield, GU31 4AA ☎ 01730 266431.

The Walk

1 Starting with the church gate on your right, walk to the bend in the road. Here, there are two footpath signs on the left. Follow the second one to keep going fairly straight ahead into the woods. The track then bears right to a metal kissing gate and into a sheep field. The path crosses a small stream, then bears left through the field to another kissing gate. Once you are through the gate, turn left, then follow the path around to the right as it follows a fence line alongside **Steep Farm**. Follow the footpath signs onto a hard track.

2 Turn left, away from Steep Farm, to follow the footpath over another small stream. Ignore the footpath to the left, and instead, briefly bear slightly right. Keep straight ahead at the next junction to take the lower left-hand footpath through the woods along the edge of a field. The footpath crosses the drive to a cottage at the **Moors** (there could be chickens here) then goes back under the trees for a short way. Ignore the next footpath sign to the left; instead, head up

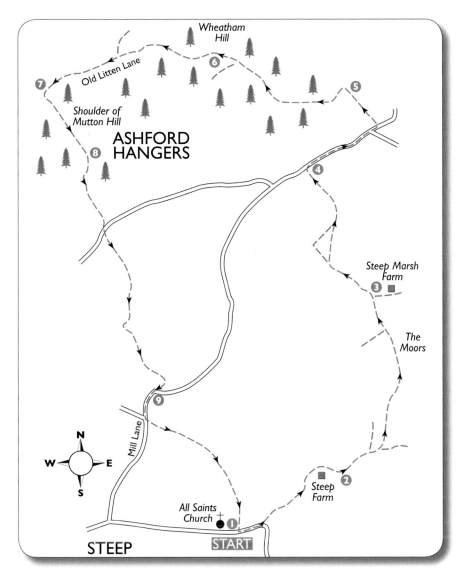

the steep slope onto a concrete area at the back of **Steep Marsh Farm**.

3 Cross the farmyard to a signpost, then turn left over a stile with a dog gate next to it. Keep following this footpath as it alternates between fields and woodland, negotiating a couple of kissing gates on the way, until you reach a road.

4 Turn right to follow this country lane for about ¼ mile until just after you pass another road coming up from the right. Soon after the road junction, turn left over a stile into the field. Take care here: the stile is set back from the road up a short bank, so it is easy to miss. Then begin the climb up towards **Ashford Hangers**, through an avenue of trees in the middle of the field. This field may contain cows or horses.

5 At the end of the avenue, cross over another stile into the nature reserve. The dogs can now have more freedom. Turn left onto the wide track of **Old Litten Lane**, and stay on this main track as it climbs **Wheatham Hill**.

At the gate to the sheep enclosure which covers the hilltop, you might want to take a short detour off the track to explore the hill. At 249 metres (817 feet), Wheatham Hill is one of the highest hills in the county of Hampshire. This is the site of Cobbett's View, the details of which are on the information panel at the gate.

6 Continue on the hard track, with the fence line on your right. Pass a wooden barrier and keep going straight ahead. At the next signpost, the **Hangers Way** joins the path from the right. Continue around a gentle curve, then turn left down the **Hangers Way** footpath.

7 Follow the route straight down **Shoulder of Mutton Hill**. Just past the bench, you will get your first glimpse of the amazing view. Beyond the bench, the hill is now bare of many of the magnificent beech trees, which were uprooted in the hurricane of 1987. On the way down to the **Poet's Stone**, there are panoramic views of the surrounding countryside and across to the **South Downs**. This is a fine place to pause for a while and admire the view.

8 Walk straight down the hillside. Note that this is very steep. After descending a flight of steps cut into the hill, follow the field edge to a lane. Doing a dog-leg to cross the lane, continue down a tarmac drive, which is still the **Hangers Way**. When the drive ends, bear half left along a path, which is usually muddy. Zigzag right and then left across a sloping meadow. Immediately after a bird hide, go right to continue on the **Hangers Way** past a waterfall to the junction with **Mill Lane**.

9 When you join the road, go straight ahead up **Mill Lane**. At the first junction, go left through a swing gate, and follow the woodland edge on your right. Then follow the footpath through the wood, bearing right at the bench and crossing the playing field to head back to the church.

Binsted
4 miles (6.4 km)

Dogs will enjoy a swim at Point 2 on the walk.

Binsted is a delightful rural Hampshire village. The walk starts in the oldest part of the village, where the church nestles between open farmland and half-timbered cottages close to the village school. The first part of the route passes through the graveyard, which is the final resting place of Field Marshal Montgomery. After passing a series of ponds, there is a steep climb up above the village, where the open, mainly arable landscape gives views across much of Hampshire. Despite the ascents, this is a fairly easy walking route, mainly along wide grass tracks and hard tracks. A sign at Point 3 asks for dogs to be kept on leads in the conservation area, but having run free since leaving the church, and enjoyed a swim, my dogs were happy to stay close for a little while.

The South Downs – A Dog Walker's Guide

How to get there & where to park

Binsted is a small village about 4 miles east of Alton in Hampshire. There is a parking area by the church, but try to avoid school pick-up times: the church is close to the primary school, and the parking gets used by parents on the school run. **Sat nav** GU34 4NX.

OS map

Explorer 144 Basingstoke, Alton & Whitchurch (GR SU 772409).

Nearest refreshments

You will pass the dog-friendly Cedars pub in Binsted at the end of the route, around a 10-minute walk from the church. GU34 4PB ☎ 01420 22112.

Dog factors

Terrain: Fairly easy walking, mainly along wide grass and hard tracks. A couple of fairly steep climbs.
Road walking: One lane crossing, and 5 minutes through the village near the end of the walk.
Livestock: Sheep in the fields either side of the short path at the very end of the walk.
Stiles: Two.
Nearest vet: Cedar Veterinary Group, Clifton Veterinary Surgery, Anstey Lane, Alton, GU34 2RH ☎ 01420 82163.

The Walk

1 Enter the churchyard by the cross, and follow the path past the front of the church. Bear slightly right onto the grass and towards the yew hedge that runs along the back of the graveyard. Keep the yew hedge on your right and cross the graveyard.

In the far-right corner of the graveyard you will pass the grave of Field Marshal Montgomery.

Leave the graveyard to follow the track in front of you across an arable field.

2 At the crossing track, turn right, then almost immediately left, to follow the marked footpath across the field. It then drops down into a small copse, where it wiggles as it goes downhill before emerging in an arable field. Turn left here, and follow the footpath along a broad grass track as it makes its way between a series of ponds and large arable fields, with great views across open countryside. My water-loving dogs enjoy this part of the route. When the footpath leaves the field and joins another tree-lined path, turn right in front of the metal gates.

(3) Here, you start the uphill part of the journey. Very soon after turning uphill, bear left off the track next to an old stile.

You are now entering a conservation area that asks for dogs to be kept on leads.

A series of steps helps with the steep incline into a field. At the top of the steps, turn left, and follow the tree line around the edge of the open farmland. You will need to be vigilant as you enjoy the level path after the climb: it is easy to miss the footpath sign that marks your sharp left turn into the tree line. This path initially takes you back on yourself as you descend a few more steps; then a narrow path takes you to the valley bottom. The footpath then turns right across grassland to a stile.

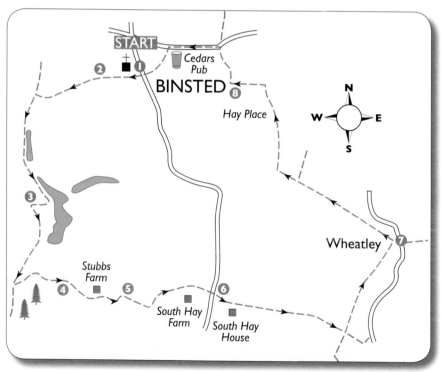

4 Over the stile, you have another climb to conquer. The path bears very slightly left in front of you to cross the arable field to the tree line opposite. When the path reaches the trees, it bears slightly right to follow the tree line, and continues uphill to **Stubbs Farm**.

This is the end of the conservation area.

5 At **Stubbs Farm**, follow the footpath to the left, and then to the right, onto the concrete farm track.

If you look to the left, you can see Binsted church spire in the distance.

Follow the farm track through a series of turns until it becomes tarmac, by **South Hay Farm**. Here, drop down to cross a country lane.

As you follow the footpath sign across the lane, you will get a glimpse of the rather splendid **South Hay House** *on your right.*

6 Having crossed the lane, the path again goes uphill, curving past a few houses. A short stretch of grassland then brings you to another stile. The route after the stile is straight ahead up the hill and over an arable field. Keeping the pylons to your right, follow the path over the brow of the hill. Soon after you start to descend, you can see a signpost, where you will turn left to follow the semi-hard track under the overhead power lines towards the houses of **Wheatley**.

7 Bear right at the metal gates so you can go through the wooden barrier onto a hard track. Turn left and follow the hard track. The track starts fairly straight, before turning right in front of a flint barn; it then winds its way along to the tarmac drive of **Hay Place**.

8 Following the footpath along the tarmac drive brings you to the road through the village. Turn left.

In a few minutes, you will reach the Cedars pub, if you fancy stopping for a little refreshment.

Passing the pub, you are soon walking alongside a high brick wall. At the end of the wall, turn left to follow the footpath between sheep fields back to the church.

Cheriton
3 miles (4.8 km)

A run at Point 2 on the walk, on the Wayfarer's Way.

The name of Cheriton means church village, and probably originates from the time of Henry of Blois, Bishop of Winchester 1129–1171, who built the church. The village is the source of the River Itchen, which can be seen as a shallow stream that crosses the very pretty village green. With thatched cottages, a 12th-century church, a stone cross and delightful weeping willows, this really is a quintessential English 'chocolate box' village.

Starting in the village, the walk follows a simple, fairly gentle route up onto downland and along old drovers' trails with views across Hampshire, returning via pasture land alongside the river and flood meadows. The small amount of road walking, and the possibility of livestock in places, mean that dogs will need to be on leads or kept close at times, but for most of the walk they can run free.

The South Downs – A Dog Walker's Guide

Dog factors

Terrain: Fairly gentle, across downland and meadows.

Road walking: Some at each end of the walk, a road crossing and a short section on the route. In total, about 1/3 mile.

Livestock: A field which may contain sheep. There may also be cows. There probably will be horses in the paddocks during the last mile.

Stiles: Two, easy to navigate for a large Labrador.

Nearest vet: Cedar Veterinary Group, The Veterinary Surgery, New Farm Road, Alresford, SO24 9QW ☎ 01962 732535.

How to get there & where to park

Cheriton is signposted from the A272. There are usually parking places in the village around the green or by the village shop. **Sat nav** SO24 0PZ.

OS map

Explorer OL32 Winchester (GR SU 582284).

Nearest refreshments

The Flower Pots in Cheriton is a lovely, award-winning, old-fashioned country pub with its own brewery. The pub is a 5-minute walk from the start of the route. SO24 0QQ ☎ 01962 771318 www.flowerpotscheriton.co.uk.

The Walk

1 Make your way to the war memorial cross on the corner of the village green, opposite the village hall. The walk starts on the road between the cross and the willow tree. With the willow on your left, turn left to follow the road alongside the stream towards a road junction. Bear left at the road signpost to cross the stream, then turn left at the footpath, just before **Cheriton House**. You are now on the **Wayfarer's Way**, which runs alongside the stream until it passes a house; here, the path turns right to follow a narrow, fenced track uphill. The Wayfarer's Way continues as a fenced track, soon leaving the houses behind. Follow the track around the field boundaries. The open farmland rewards you for the climb with extensive views across Hampshire.

2 When you reach a crossroads, where the **Wayfarer's Way** is crossed by the **Itchen Way**, stay on the **Wayfarer's Way** as it continues straight ahead to follow the restricted bridleway. When the bridleway drops down to a sunken track at another crossroads, leave the Wayfarer's Way, turning left to follow the bridleway down **Broad Lane**. Just after a cowshed, the bridleway crosses **Badshear Lane**; though this is marked on the OS map as a road, it isn't tarmacked and appears to be just another wide track.

3 Going straight over **Badshear Lane**, continue to follow the wide track of the bridleway. Ignore another bridleway joining from your left, and continue straight ahead. Shortly your track narrows as it goes uphill through some trees. Towards the top of the hill you will come to another signpost junction. This time, turn left downhill, towards the road.

4 At the road, go straight over onto the lane to **Titchfield**. After crossing a number of streams, turn left between the brick buildings of **Cheriton Mill**.

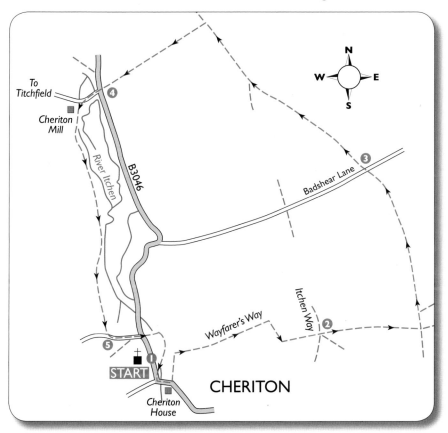

The South Downs – A Dog Walker's Guide

Follow the fence line, with the river on your left. You are back on the **Wayfarer's Way**. There are now 4 fields to cross, which involves negotiating a couple of easy stiles. There are occasionally some tame ponies in the last field, who may have to be asked to move so you can get to the gate.

5 When you get to a hard-surfaced lane next to a barn on your left, turn left down the lane. Follow the lane down to the road through the village. Cross the road towards the **Wayfarer's Way signpost**, then bear right along the lane past the thatched cottages and the village shop and back to the cross on the village green.

Droxford
3 miles (4.8 km)

The water meadow at Droxford.

Droxford is a delightful village in Hampshire's Meon Valley. The first historical record of the village is from when the manor of *Drocenesforda* – Droxford's ancient name – was granted to the prior and monks of St Swithun, Winchester, by King Egbert in 826. Despite the busy A32 running through it, it still manages to retain the feel and charm of a country village. This isn't the shortest route in the book, but it is probably the easiest. It is ideal for a good family amble when the longer or more undulating routes would put some family members off.

The doggy car park etiquette of putting the leads on before you get the dogs out of the car is advisable, as you park close to the A-road. Leads would be polite at the start of the walk along the Wayfarer's Way, as it goes through the pretty yard of the Norman church of St Mary and All Saints. Just past the church, the route crosses the River Meon, then follows its course through water meadows until you reach the Meon Valley Trail. The dogs can run free all the way on this long-distance path, which links West Meon with Wickham. The path is a delightful example of nature reclaiming an artificial environment, in this case a disused railway line. The way home takes you back over the river past an old watermill, before returning to the church to complete a circuit of Droxford.

How to get there & where to park

Droxford lies 5 miles east of Bishop's Waltham. From the A32, drive into the centre of the village. There is a car park by the village hall, just off Droxford High Street. **Sat nav** SO32 3PA.

OS map

Explorer OL32 Winchester (GR SU 606182).

Nearest refreshments

The award-winning Bakers Arms in Droxford is a delightful free house serving good food. There is a car park, but the pub is only a few minutes' walk from the start of the route. SO32 3PA ☎ 01489 877533 www.thebakersarmsdroxford.com.

Dog factors

Terrain: Fairly flat. Very easy grass or semi-hard tracks. As may be expected, the water meadows can get muddy, but even at the end of a very wet winter they were not bad.

Road walking: Crossing a bridge, and a few hundred metres down a quiet lane.

Livestock: Possible in the water meadows. There may be horses on the Meon Valley Trail.

Stiles: Two, both passable by a large Labrador. You may not have to use them: the fence had been taken down next to the first, and the gate next to the second isn't usually locked. The kissing gates, however, are quite tight for a large dog if they are not used to them.

Nearest vet: Shield Veterinary Centre, Victoria Road, Bishop's Waltham, Southampton, SO32 1DJ ☎ 01489 896734.

The Walk

. . . .

1 From the back of the car park, follow the sign for the **Wayfarer's Way**. Walk through the churchyard, swing right, passing a gate on your left, and walk around the end of the church. Turn left out of the churchyard, and within a few metres, cross a very pretty stream over a footbridge. A water meadow takes you to a second bridge over the **River Meon**; cross this bridge, too.

2 Just past the second footbridge, turn right with the **Wayfarer's Way** through a kissing gate, then follow the river along the bottom of the field to another gate. As you cross the next field, the river begins to swing away to your right, but you keep going straight ahead. When you reach a field boundary hedge, the Wayfarer's Way is joined by a footpath. Stay on the **Wayfarer's Way** as it veers slightly left and gently uphill towards a small copse of mature trees. At the back of the copse, you can see the railway embankment. You will now be walking parallel with the embankment until you leave the water meadows. Through the trees, you reach a stile, the fence to the right of which has been removed to allow cattle access to a feeding station within the copse of trees. Keep to the slightly higher ground as you continue along the water meadows towards a bridge.

3 As you approach the bridge, you can see it carries a lane over the river, which has swung back up the meadow to meet you. Going up a slope to the left of the bridge, negotiate another kissing gate onto the lane (**Cutts Arch**). Turn left on the lane, then cross another bridge, this time over the disused railway line.

The railway came to Droxford in 1903 with the building of the Meon Valley Railway. A station was built around ½ mile outside the village, on the other side of the river. A small sub-settlement grew around the station, including a hotel, railway workers' cottages and a cluster of private homes. British Railways closed the railway in 1962.

Immediately after crossing the railway bridge, turn left by a signpost. With a wooden fence on your left, follow a narrow track initially above, then dropping down to meet, the **Meon Valley Trail** on the railway track. Ambling along this delightful shady track, you can see across the water meadow you just left. Pass a raised path to your left, where there is a bench just before you go under a bridge. You might like to make a small detour to read the notice next to the bench.

In June 1944, Allied leaders including Churchill, Eisenhower and de Gaulle met in a train carriage at Droxford station to discuss the imminent D-Day invasion. This bench commemorates the meeting of world leaders.

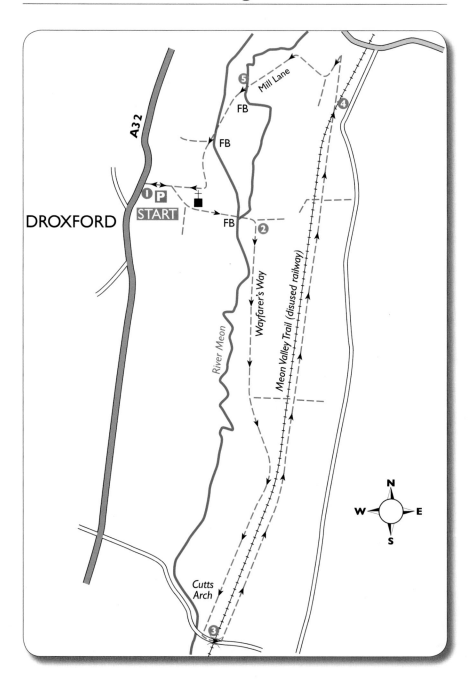

4 When you reach a green wooden fence on your right, you have arrived at the platform for the old railway station. Keep following the fence line until you reach a footpath sign next to a '**no parking**' sign. Turn left, then immediately left again, so you are walking back in the direction you have just come from, this time following a narrow path through the trees. Very soon, you reach a junction, where you turn right to follow a fenced track downhill to **Mill Lane**. Turn left onto a very quiet dead-end lane, where the tarmac ends just before the river. Luckily, you won't have to get your feet wet, as there is a footbridge.

5 Having negotiated the bridge, follow a narrow path as it winds with the river, passing over the spillway of the mill to arrive at a tarmac drive. Turn left in a few strides as the drive turns right, and keep straight ahead to a stile by a gate – you will usually find the gate unlocked, if you would prefer not to negotiate the stile. Once through the gate or over the stile, you are in a small paddock. Go straight ahead from the stile, and you will soon see the church to your right. Another kissing gate takes you back onto the **Wayfarer's Way** in the churchyard, where you retrace your steps back to the car park.

The Meon Valley Trail.

Owslebury to Marwell
6 miles (9.7 km)

Just off Pitcot Lane at Point 1.

Owslebury is a delightful rural village with a quiet, relaxed atmosphere, just 5 miles from Winchester. The route starts at the pretty church, and passes thatched cottages and flint buildings. From the glebe field next to the church, the views extend to the Isle of Wight. This peaceful route is slightly interrupted mid-walk when the sounds of children having fun at Marwell Activity Centre can be heard on your way around the perimeter of the zoo. The zoo is in the grounds of Marwell Hall, thought to be the scene of the courtship and subsequent secret marriage of Henry VIII and Lady Jane Seymour in 1536.

How to get there & where to park
Owslebury is signposted from the A272, and is around 5 miles from Winchester. However, the price of a lovely rural village is limited parking. There is a little parking outside the church and a car park by the village hall, but the latter requires permission ☎ 01962 777354. Alternatively, you could park outside the pub if you are planning on visiting. It's on the route, so you can make an easy adjustment and start the walk at Point 10 instead. **Sat nav** SO21 1LN (for Point 1).

OS map
Explorer OL3 Meon Valley (GR SU 515234).

Nearest refreshments
Dogs will receive a warm welcome in the bar or large garden at the Ship Inn in Owslebury. SO21 1LT ☎ 01962 777756.

Dog factors

Terrain: On the whole, the going is good and the hills are gentle. The bridleway near the zoo can get very wet in the winter.
Road walking: A couple of road crossings; two short sections on a quiet lane and through the village. Around ½ mile in total.
Livestock: None directly on the route, but you do pass fields which may contain some. There may be horses on the bridleways.
Stiles: Two. The gate is usually open next to the first; the second is next to a post and rail, and is easily negotiated by large Labradors.
Nearest vet: Unicorn Vets, Fairfield Surgery, Winchester Road, Fair Oak, Eastleigh, SO50 7GW ☎ 02380 601900.

The Walk

1 From the church, walk through the kissing gate into the graveyard, and bear left to follow the footpath through a little gate down some steps to **Pitcot Lane**. Turn right to join the combined routes of two well-marked long-distance paths, the **Monarch's Way** and the **Pilgrims' Trail**. Follow them for the next 1½ miles. The path is a mixture of stony or grass tracks and woodland paths. You will negotiate a couple of kissing gates and an easy stile, and cross **Lower Baybridge Lane**. The route takes you across open fields with extensive views and then through some enclosed woodland.

2 As you emerge out of a deer-fenced woodland enclosure through a tall kissing gate, turn left, then immediately right, to continue following the long-distance paths down the hard track of a road used as a public path. Follow this straight track along the edge of the downland fields for about ¼ mile.

3 When the long-distance paths turn left across the fields, continue on the hard track. A couple of paces further down the road, turn right to follow the yellow arrow of a footpath around the fence line of another enclosed woodland. At the end of the fence line, the footpath turns left into an arable field, then continues to follow the fence line. Stay with the fence line when it turns left again by a tree and a wooden barrier. Keep to the grass track alongside the fence.

*If you look across the field to your right, you can see **Marwell House**.*

4 At the end of the tree line, turn right to follow a footpath towards the sheep fields of **Marwell Farm**. Over the stile, or through the wooden fence for the dogs, you are now on an enclosed track between livestock fields. The footpath heads towards the buildings, then swings right between them, before emerging on a hard drive, where you turn left to follow the drive to **Whaddon Lane**.

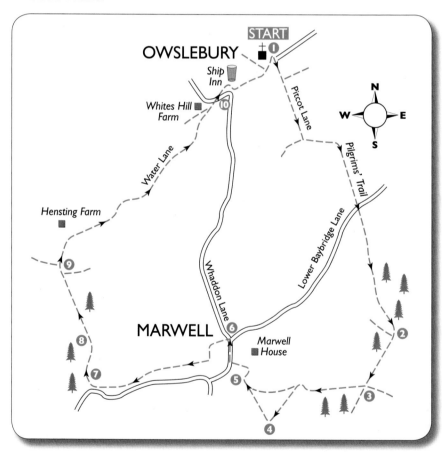

5 There is now a little road walking. Turn right onto **Whaddon Lane**, and pass the rather grand entrance to **Marwell House**. Ahead, you can see a road junction where **Whaddon Lane** turns left as it meets **Lower Baybridge Lane**. Stay on **Whaddon Lane** until just past the junction. Looking left across the lane, you can see a large metal gate. Cross the lane towards the gate to reach the boundary fence of **Marwell Zoo**.

6 Take the bridleway to the left of the gate, and start the journey around the zoo's perimeter. The bridleway starts outside the boundary fence, then swings left uphill to briefly leave it. Back on level ground, the path turns right to rejoin the boundary fence. Keep the zoo fence on your right, crossing **South Road** (the zoo's access road). The bridleway follows the boundary all the way to the zoo's car park.

The bridleway can get very wet in the winter, but for most of the way, there is an alternative narrow track through the woods to your left.

7 When the bridleway meets a road junction, it swings right before crossing the pedestrian entrance/exit to the zoo. The bridleway continues onto a gravel track between the boundary fence and the car park. Again, this part of the bridleway can be very wet. A short diversion into the car park, then a right turn, will allow you to follow its course to the end of the car park.

8 At the end of the car park, the bridleway crosses the track to the overflow car park, then continues straight ahead back into the woods. Very shortly, you'll come to a junction by a wooden gate. Pass the gate on your right, and continue straight towards **Horsham Copse**. Stay with the bridleway, ignoring both the footpath that crosses into the meadow on your left and the next bridleway on your right.

9 When the bridleway you are on meets a Y-junction, bear right to follow the edge of the wood slightly uphill. You are now following **Water Lane**, which, despite its name, is usually dry. The tree-lined lane swings right at the boundary of **Hensting Farm**, then meanders its way gently uphill to **Owslebury**.

10 When you reach a post in the middle of the track, keep the dogs close, as the bridleway soon passes **Whites Hill Farm**. Bear right onto a hard track to arrive at the junction with **Whites Hill**. Bear right onto **Whites Hill**, and you will soon be in front of the **Ship Inn**. With the pub front door on your left, keep left on **Main Road** to walk through the village back to the church and your car.

St Catherine's Hill to Twyford Down

4¼ miles (6.8 km)

St Catherine's Hill.

St **Catherine's Hill is a haven** for wild flowers and butterflies, and is managed by the Wildlife Trust. It is also part of the East Hampshire Area of Outstanding Natural Beauty. The top of this chalk hill is ringed by the ramparts of an Iron Age hillfort, and there are the remains of a Norman chapel hidden under the beech trees. The summit is also home to the Winchester Mizmaze, one of only eight surviving historic English turf mazes. The views to Winchester, the cathedral and across the Itchen Valley are spectacular.

This is the most urban walk in the book, but there is plenty of countryside to enjoy, with ancient chalk pastures, a peaceful river and shady woodland, along with an abundance of fauna and flora. For a lot of the walk, the dogs will need to be kept close or on leads. Dogs that like a good sniff rather than a good gallop will have more freedom, but there are places on the route for both. This is such an interesting and varied walk the dogs seemed to enjoy it as much as we did.

How to get there & where to park

From the south, take Junction 10 off the M3, then take the first exit at the roundabout. Immediately after the bridge, turn left into Garnier Road car park. From the north, take Junction 9 off the M3, and take the A31 south. Pass under the motorway, and at the roundabout, take the first exit; immediately after the bridge, turn left into the small car park. **Sat nav** SO23 9PA.

OS map

Explorer OL32 Winchester (GR SU 483280).

Nearest refreshments

The hillfort is ideal for a picnic, or the Bell Inn on St Cross Road is a lovely, dog-friendly pub. SO23 9RE ☎ 01962 865284 www.thebellstcross.co.uk.

Dog factors

Terrain: Varies from tarmac, chalk and flint to woodland and grassland paths. May be muddy in places, and can be slippery in the wet. Some ups and downs, with steps at the steepest parts.
Road walking: A few metres on a pavement and a couple of road crossings – one a major one with a pelican crossing. The route goes under the M3 on the way out and over it on the way back.
Livestock: Cows and/or sheep within the nature reserves for the last mile.
Stiles: One, coming off the golf course, which could be easily bypassed.
Nearest vet: Stable Close Veterinary Clinic, 39B St Cross Road, Winchester, SO23 9PR ☎ 01962 840505.

The Walk

1 From the car park, with the disused railway bridge and line to your left, follow the tarmac footpath along the **Itchen Way** alongside the river.

There is plenty to see along this path, with views across the river, an interesting stone carving in the shape of a boat, and trees with visible root systems that keep them from sliding down the railway embankment.

Pass the gate into the wildlife reserve. Walk under another disused railway bridge, and soon you will come to a junction.

For their safety, have the dogs on leads now.

Go straight on at this junction; soon you will reach the very busy A3090.

2 Turn left just before the end of the path. You are now on the pavement by a pelican crossing. Cross the A3090 using the crossings, then turn right along the pavement for a few metres to a footpath sign. Turn left at the sign to go under the M3. The footpath runs along the towpath for the **Itchen Navigation**. After crossing a wooden footbridge, turn left, and follow the path to a B-road opposite **Hockley Golf Course**.

3 Cross directly over the road into the golf course car park, and turn right. Keep walking until you pass some buildings, then turn left to follow the footpath uphill on a chalk track, so beginning our ascent of **Twyford Down**. Bear left around a white sign telling you to keep to the footpath. The slightly undulating footpath wiggles along through some trees, then uphill, to emerge on a plateau next to a signpost.

4 Turn right towards a stile at the edge of the golf course. (There is a gap next to it, so it may be less effort to ignore the stile and squeeze through the gap.) Turn left at the signpost to join the bridleway, which runs around the outskirts of the golf course. After a few gentle turns, the bridleway runs fairly straight until you get to a crossroads.

5 Turn left to join the **Pilgrims' Trail**. The path goes up through some trees, crossing **Twyford Down**. The route follows the top boundary of the golf course on your left, with open farmland on your right. Soon you will get views to the city. Continue to follow the **Pilgrims' Trail** through the gate into the wildlife enclosure (this may contain livestock) where you start your descent of the **Downs**.

6 Through the gate at the bottom of the enclosure, turn left over the motorway. Go through the gate into **St Catherine's Hill**. Follow the bridleway down through the valley, and you will soon lose the noise of the motorway. Now you have a choice. Either continue down the valley to the steps up to the entrance to the Iron Age fort, or turn right and follow any of the paths that meander up the hill to the path that runs along the ramparts of the fort. Here, turn left, with the rampart on your right and the valley bottom below. This path will take you to the top of the steps and the entrance to the fort.

7 Go through the entrance to the fort, and follow the track ahead. You should have the hilltop to your left and the rampart to your right. The track follows the slight curve of the hilltop, then turns left around the edge of 'the **Clump**'

– a small copse of beech trees which hides the remains of a Norman chapel. The path crosses the hilltop between the Clump and the **Mizmaze**.

❽ Walk past the turf maze to a noticeboard. Again, you have a choice of routes. The shortest way back to the car park is straight down the hill from the noticeboard, bearing right, then left, to go through the gate by the railway bridge. Under the bridge, you are back at the car park. This route is steep and can be slippery in wet weather. The alternative, longer route is to turn left at the noticeboard and walk around the top of the hill back to the fort entrance. Descend using the steps, then bear right to follow the bridleway through the gates out of the enclosure and back onto the **Itchen Way**. Turn right to retrace your outward journey back to the car park.

OTHER TITLES FROM COUNTRYSIDE BOOKS

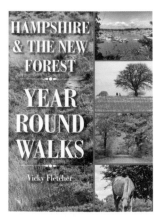

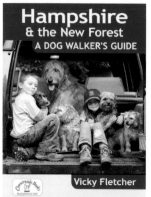

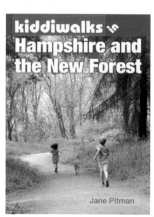

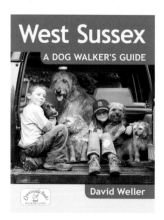

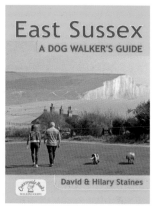

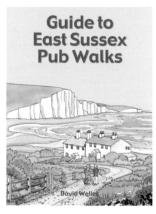

To see the full range of books by Countryside Books please visit
www.countrysidebooks.co.uk

Follow us on